GROWING WEARY DOING GOOD?

Encouragement for Exhau

KARLA WORLEY

New Hope® Publishers
Birmingham, Alabama

New Hope® Publishers
P.O. Box 12065
Birmingham, AL 35202-2065
www.newhopepubl.com

Library of Congress Cataloging-in-Publication Data

Worley, Karla.
Growing Weary Doing Good? Encouragement for Exhausted Women / Karla Worley.
     p. cm.
Includes bibliographical references.
ISBN 1-56309-438-X

   1. Christian women—Religious life.
   2. Encouragement—Religious aspects—Christianity. I. Title.

BV4527 .W63 2001
248.8'43—dc21
00-012052

Cover design by Rachael Crutchfield
Cover photo by Ralph Anderson

ISBN: 1-56309-438-X
N014112•0301•7.5M1

FOR THE BELOVEDS

Be assured
that from the first day we heard of you,
we haven't stopped praying for you, asking God to give you
wise minds and spirits attuned to his will,
and so acquire a thorough understanding of the ways
in which God works.

We pray that you'll live well for the Master,
making him proud of you as you work hard in his orchard.
As you learn more and more how God works,
you will learn how to do your work.

We pray that you'll have the strength to stick it out
over the long haul—not the grim strength
of gritting your teeth
but the glory-strength God gives.
It is strength that endures the unendurable
and spills over into joy,
thanking the Father who makes us
strong enough to take part
in everything bright and beautiful that he has for us.

—Colossians 1:9–11
The Message

TABLE OF CONTENTS

Growing Weary in Doing Good

Let us not grow weary in doing good, for at the proper time, we will reap a harvest if we do not give up.

—Galatians 6:9

The church has become an organization of well-meaning idealists, working for Christ, but far from his presence and power.

—Flora Wuellner[1]

*T*he year began with a bang . . . literally. I woke from a mid-afternoon nap, feeling as if someone were sitting on my chest. Pain radiated down my left arm. I was dizzy. It was hard to breathe.

My husband rushed me to the hospital. Hooked to electrodes, I lay in the emergency room listening to the beep, beep, beep of multiple heart monitors at the nurse's station outside my curtain. Periodically a machine would go haywire, and I could hear the nurse say, "Arrhythmia in 13!" All I could think was, *Am I in 13? Am I in 13?*

I wasn't. And I hadn't had a heart attack. I had had a panic attack.

"Bring in your calendar," my doctor said. "That's what we need to treat."

Following his assessment of my condition and his prescription for my recovery, I canceled my commitments for the next two months, farmed out my kids to neighbors and friends, and lay down to "rest." That's when I discovered that "rest" involves more than taking a nap. Although my body was still, my mind raced; and my heart raced even faster. My soul needed rest.

An old preacher's story goes like this: A small country church voted to refurbish their sanctuary. Wishing to be frugal, the deacons decided to paint the walls themselves. They carefully calculated their budget and purchased the necessary supplies. Early on a Saturday morning, they began to paint. As the day passed, it became clear that the deacons had not bought enough paint for the entire job, so they began to thin the remaining supply of paint. As the job stretched on, the paint grew thinner and thinner. By evening, the deacons were done, the sanctuary was tidied, and the lights were turned out for the night.

When the congregation arrived the next morning, they were dismayed at the results. With the sun streaming through the sanctuary windows, the thinned-out paint was streaky, and the old paint was showing through. The preacher took his place behind the pulpit and studied the walls for a moment. He then turned to the deacons, pointed his finger, and declared, "Repaint! Repaint! Thin no more!"

I must confess I have often spread myself so thin that I was of no more use than the deacons' paint job. I grew up in the church, so I learned early to respond to the call to "serve the Lord and His church." At one point, I found myself singing in the adult choir, teaching a Sunday school class, presiding over a missions organization, leading children's choir, and serving on two church committees! At about this time I found myself in the emergency room, falling to pieces. This may be the only way some committees will allow you to resign your position! If this ever happens to you, my advice is to keep your bathrobe on as long as possible. As soon as you get dressed, everyone assumes you're well.

I don't think I'm alone in this. As I speak to Christian women around the country, I look into their eyes and recognize the signs of exhaustion. We are worn out—not only physically and mentally, but spiritually as well.

"There is almost universal belief in the immense difficulty of being a *real* Christian," writes professor and theologian Dallas Willard. "We believe in our hearts that we should be Christlike, closely following our Lord. However, few of us, if any, can see this as a real possibility for ourselves or others we know well."[2]

Is the Christian life really so difficult? Or have we misinterpreted what is meant by "the Christian life"? Are we so exhausted because Christ requires so much, or because we don't understand what He truly requires?

In Galatians 6:9, Paul exhorted the young believers in Galatia, "Let us not grow weary in doing good, for at the proper time, we will reap a harvest if we do not give up." *The Message* paraphrase reads, "Let us not allow ourselves to become fatigued." Our churches are full of fatigued people. We are not just fatigued by the pace of life; we are fatigued by the pace of *church* life. We are perilously in danger of becoming so weary from "doing church" that we will grow weary of it and give up.

But take a closer look at Galatians 6:9. It does not say "doing church"; it says "doing good." This word *doing* comes from the Greek *poieo*. It means "producing," as in "bringing forth," "bearing a result"—the way a tree produces fruit. Does a tree bear fruit because it tries really hard? Does a flower bloom because it labors to produce a bud? No! This is silly. The fruit and the flower are not the result of anything the plant does. They are a result of what the plant is—how God created it. The resulting crop is determined by the nature of the seed that is planted. Apple seeds produce apples.

Dandelion seeds produce dandelions. "Do people pick grapes from thornbushes, or figs from thistles?" Jesus asked. "Likewise every good tree bears good fruit, but a bad tree bears bad fruit" (Matt. 7:17).

The word *good, kalos* in Greek, means "pleasing" or "beautiful." What is beautiful to God? Here are some Scriptures that use this Greek word *kalos* and its Hebrew counterpart *tob*:

- God saw all that he had made, and it was very good (Gen. 1:31).
- Good and upright is the LORD (Psalm 25:8).
- Taste and see that the LORD is good (Psalm 34:8).
- But as for me, it is good to be near God (Psalm 73:28).
- I know that nothing good lives in me, that is, in my sinful nature. For I have the desire to do what is good, but I cannot carry it out (Rom. 7:18).
- Everything God created is good (1 Tim. 4:4).

Clearly, the word *good* here has nothing to do with deeds. It has to do with God's nature. His nature, reproduced in us, is beautiful and pleasing to Him. The fruit of the Spirit listed in Galatians 5:22 are characteristics of God's nature: God is loving, joyful, peaceful, patient, kind, good, faithful, gentle, and self-controlled. The problem is, we are not any of these things by nature. It is no wonder that we become fatigued trying to act lovingly, patiently, kindly, gently—no surprise we are exhausted from trying to exhibit joy, peace, goodness, faithfulness, and self-control, since we can no more sweat and strain to produce these qualities than a thistle can produce grapes! And yet, there it is: Paul challenges believers, "Let us not allow ourselves to become fatigued in producing what is beautiful."

How on earth are we going to bring forth what is not in our nature to bear? We must get a new nature. This is what Jesus meant when He told Nicodemus that a man must be born again

(John 3:3). Before Paul talked about producing this good fruit, he explained how it would be possible. "I no longer live; but Christ lives in me" (Gal. 2:20). "In fact," Paul continued, "I have been set free from being busy for God. Instead, God is busy in me."

"Since this is the kind of life we have chosen," Paul exhorted, "let us make sure that we do not just hold it as an idea in our heads or a sentiment in our hearts, but work out its implications in every detail of our lives" (Gal. 5:25 *The Message*).

The Christian life is the very real process of God producing His nature in us. Every day, in every detail of our lives, "He must become greater; I must become less" (John 3:30). "It is God who works in you to will and to act according to his good purpose," Paul wrote to the Philippians (2:13). Who's doing the work here? God. God is doing the good—not us. Don't miss this. It is easy to be so busy trying to produce *for* God that our lives produce very little *of* God. But "if our Christian journey does not produce Christ in us," writes Brennan Manning, "if the passing years do not form Jesus in us in such a way that we really resemble him, our spirituality is bankrupt."[3]

Ouch. This may hurt. But don't despair. "Learn as you go along what pleases the Lord," advised Paul (Eph. 5:10 TLB). We continually adapt to this new nature and its implications in every detail of our lives. Only in heaven will we fully understand and accept God's ways and His timetable.

"For at the proper time," Paul continued in Galatians 6:9, "we will reap a harvest if we do not give up." The phrase "the proper time" comes from the Greek root word *idios*, which is literally translated "one's own" or "belonging to himself" or "distinctive." From it we get the words *idiom* (a style or expression unique to a culture) and *idiosyncrasy* (a distinctive behavior or habit particular to one person—my son Ben's gravelly laugh, the way my friend Gigi pins a silk flower to her blouse, or the way I always leave the tag sticking up in the back of mine). The "proper" time is "God's own" time—the time that belongs solely to Him. "I choose the appointed time," God said in Psalm 75:2.

Throughout the Bible's narrative, there is constant reference to God's distinctive ownership and management of time:

- 🌿 I will return to you at the appointed time next year and Sarah will have a son (Gen. 18:14).
- 🌿 You will arise and have compassion on Zion, for it is time to show favor to her; the appointed time has come (Psalm 102:13).
- 🌿 Jesus told His disciples, "I am not yet going up to this Feast, because for me the right time has not yet come" (John 7:8).
- 🌿 You see, at just the right time, when we were still powerless, Christ died for the ungodly (Rom. 5:6).
- 🌿 When the time had fully come, God sent his Son (Gal. 4:4).

Only God knows when the time is right for the harvest, when the fruit He is producing is fully complete and ripe.

"In His time, in His time, He makes all things beautiful in His time."[4] Have you ever sung this song of praise? Unlike us, God doesn't grow tired of tending what He is growing. Do you remember, as a child, planting a seed in a paper cup of dirt and placing it in the kitchen window? I rarely ever saw anything grow from those seeds at our house; I was too impatient. I either forgot to water them, or I kept digging them up to see if they were growing yet. We humans want to see results; we want instant fruit. Even instant pudding is too slow. But God is patient. In His own time, God produces in us a harvest that is pleasing and beautiful to Him. What an encouraging promise!

But there is one condition: "We do not give up" (Gal. 6:9).

I have one more Greek word for you—the word for "give up"—and it makes me laugh. It is *ekluo*, which literally means "to loosen out of"—the way a bolt loosens out of place, as in "She must have a screw loose!" It also means "to dissolve." Paul is saying, "Let's not allow ourselves to become fatigued in producing what is pleasing to God, for in God's own time, He will produce a harvest, if we do not fall apart or dissolve." What a picture! Raise your hand if you can relate. I hear you out there, saying, "That's me! I'm falling apart." That's me, too. Or I should say, it was me.

I don't want to continue down this tiresome path. Do you? I don't want to drag myself back to the church week after week, tired when I arrive, and drag myself home, even more weary from "serving the Lord." No wonder people are reluctant to join the church! No sooner do they walk the aisle than we sign them up to teach, sing, give, go, bake, do. In church lingo, the word *service* is too often a code word for slavery. I don't want that. Do you?

Well, neither does God. Here's what He has to say about it:

> Bel bows down, Nebo stoops low; their idols are borne by beasts of burden. The images that are carried about are burdensome, a burden for the weary. They stoop and bow down together; unable to rescue the burden, they themselves go off into captivity.
>
> Listen to me, O house of Jacob, all you who remain of the house of Israel, you whom I have upheld since you were conceived, and have carried since your birth. Even to your old age and gray hairs I am he, I am he who will sustain you. I have made you and I will carry you; I will sustain you and I will rescue you (Isa. 46:1–4).

The difference between the true God and the gods of the nations is that the true God carries, and the other gods must be carried. God serves; they must be served. God glorifies His might by showing mercy. They glorify theirs by gathering slaves.[5] Our God does not want or need slaves. Jesus rebuked the Pharisees: "And you experts in the law, woe to you, because you load people down with burdens they can hardly carry, and you yourselves will not lift one finger to help them" (Luke 11:46).

For some of you, this picture is all too real. You are so weary from the burden of all you are trying to do and from the load of guilt for all you are not doing. You feel as though you have been saddled with responsibilities you can hardly carry, and no one will lift a finger to help you. I understand. God understands. And He has never intended for it to be this way.

"His pleasure is not in the strength of the horse, nor his delight in the legs of a man," declares Psalm 147:10–11. "The LORD delights in those who fear him, who put their hope in his unfailing love." We often take pride in our own strength, but God does not share our point of view. "No king is saved by the size of his army; no warrior escapes by his great strength," says Psalm 33:16. God intends for us to need Him. It's no surprise to Him that we are exhausted. He made us, and He did not create us to be fully capable on our own. For what is lacking in us drives us to Him. It pleases Him to display His strength in our weakness (2 Cor. 12:9). Did you catch that? It is beautiful to God when we are weak, because then His strength can be manifest in our lives.

I am a card-carrying member of the "Can Do" club, so this is hard for me. My friends have threatened to tattoo "Just Say No!" on my forearm. (One friend suggested that this book come with a press-on tattoo enclosed for the reader! That means you!) I have always wielded my busy schedule like a badge of honor, even though it really felt more like a ball and chain. But I am coming to realize that my friend Beth Moore is right when she says in her book *Breaking Free*, "I rarely meet a person who has come to trust God fully without painfully confronting the fact that she can't trust herself."[6]

This happened to Gideon. (See Judges 7.) On the eve of a battle with the Midianites, Gideon received some unusual instructions: "The LORD said to Gideon, 'You have too many men for me to deliver Midian into their hands. In order that Israel may not boast against me that her own strength has saved her, announce now to the people, "Anyone who trembles with fear may turn back and leave Mount Gilead."' So twenty-two thousand men left, while ten thousand remained" (Judg. 7:2–3).

Just in case Gideon forgot who was producing the results, God reduced his army by more than two-thirds. Furthermore, notice who is speaking: the LORD. That's capital L O-R-D, which is the way the New International Version of the Bible renders the name "I AM," the name God gave when Moses asked God's name (Ex. 3:13).

"I AM the One who will deliver you," God answered Moses. "I AM the One who will win the battle," God said to Gideon, "and don't you forget it!"

God prefers us in a place of weakness so that He may display His strength. One of the reasons He allows us to grow weary under our own strength is so that we will rely on Him instead of ourselves. "Therefore I will boast all the more gladly about my weaknesses," wrote the Apostle Paul, "so that Christ's power may rest on me" (2 Cor. 12:9).

The church of our time, like the church of New Testament times, must stop placing heavy burdens on people's backs—the burdens of "have to," "should have," "ought to," and the guilty load of "try harder." The church must stop requiring, as a condition for acceptance, the good works of love, joy, peace, patience, kindness, gentleness, goodness, faithfulness, and self-control; but instead should abandon itself to the I AM who places His nature in willing hearts and produces the resulting fruit. We must stop taking pride in ourselves as Strong People, and begin presenting ourselves as weak people who have a Strong and Mighty God. Just as in New Testament days, it is not the institution of the church Jesus reproves, but the individuals who make up the church. It is not some nameless "they" who create the burdens under which we labor; we ourselves do. We are the church. We are the ones who must identify the gospel of "try harder" as a false gospel.

"You foolish Galatians!" Paul wrote. "I would like to learn just one thing from you: Did you receive the Spirit by observing the law, or by believing what you heard? Are you so foolish? After beginning with the Spirit, are you now trying to attain your goal by human effort?" (Gal. 3:1–3).

We cannot live the life of Christ through our human effort, any more than we can receive the life of Christ through our human effort. Remember the relief you felt when you admitted that you needed Christ as your Savior? Believers often describe their salvation experience as "the weight of the world being lifted" from their shoulders. Remember how good it felt to lay down the burden of trying to "be good enough" and admit that only Christ can make you righteous? This is the gospel of grace.

"Restore to me the joy of your salvation," David prayed (Psalm 51:12). One version reads, "Give me the joy of your saving help again."[7] Receiving God's help is a joyous thing. There is no other way to have this new life. Why, then, do we live as though He expects us to "take it from there" on our own? When we do this, we cheat ourselves out of the joy of receiving His saving help day after day. God's grace is not only the way to salvation, but the way of life for those who are being sanctified. We become His by grace, and we become more like Him by grace. He alone can finish this task, and it is not tiresome to Him.

However, we do have some responsibility. As in salvation, the first step in receiving God's free gift of grace is this: we must want it. We must want the life of God more than we want our own way of life. We must want this burden off our shoulders and we must ask.

"We must recognize the difference between burdens that are

right for us to bear and burdens that are wrong," wrote Oswald Chambers in *My Utmost for His Highest*. "If we set out to serve God and do His work but get out of touch with Him, the sense of responsibility we feel will be overwhelming and defeating. But if we will only roll back on God the burdens He has placed on us, He will take away that immense feeling of responsibility, replacing it with an awareness and understanding of Himself and His presence."[8]

My husband, Dennis, and I used to travel together frequently. I would always tote too much luggage. Dennis would notice me lugging my heavy bag through the airport. "Want to trade?" he'd ask. What a relief to carry his light duffel instead of my bulging suitcase. Imagine the relief that comes with the exchange God offers us. He will take the responsibilities and burdens, giving us His presence instead. "You will fill me with joy in your presence," assures Psalm 16:11—the joy of accepting His saving help, the joy of knowing that I AM is with us, the God who cares and carries.

"Humble yourselves, therefore, under God's mighty hand, that he may lift you up in due time. Cast all your anxiety on him because he cares for you" (1 Peter 5:6–7). The Apostle Peter wrote these terms using images from the life he knew best: fishing. In Peter's time, fishermen would cast their nets off the boat into the sea, dredging the waters for fish. They did not toss their nets or drop their nets into the water; they cast them—hurling them as far out from the boat as they could. Peter is offering a vivid illustration of what we are to do with our burdens. Do not lay them down or half-heartedly drop them at Jesus' feet. Cast them! Hurl them! Fling them as far away from you as you can. The first step toward freedom from weariness is to say, "Get these burdens off me! I no longer want to live like this."

Of course, the opposite of this promise is also true: If you do not humble yourself, He will not lift you up. If you do not cast your anxiety on Him, you will remain exhausted. You will not know the joy of His saving help or His presence. "All forms of life have a harvest," Edith Schaeffer wisely observed.[9] I have gleaned firsthand the harvest of a too-busy life, of trying to produce for God under my own strength. I know what it is like to crash and burn. Physically, emotionally, and spiritually, I had to "lie down" for some time, and then I had to learn to stand on shaky legs and slowly begin to walk again. Sue Bender tells a similar story:

> A couple of years ago a friend of mine fell off a bike and hurt her knee. She and her husband were hiking in a national park and she could only walk very slowly. She discovered her slowed pace helped her look at the world as if through a microscope.
>
> Right behind them was a single hiker with a big camera. Every time my friend stopped to examine a wildflower, he would stop and look at the wildflower too—as if she were discovering something for him. Finally the hiker came up to her and said, "You're noticing so many wonderful things."
>
> "I'm seeing these wonderful things," she told him, "because I can't walk very fast."[10]

Perhaps you are reading this book because, like me, you've started coming loose at the seams and have ended up bedridden. Perhaps a friend gave you this book and said, "You need this!" Perhaps you saw it on the bookshelf and it screamed, "Read me!" At first I thought that we might need to package it in a plain, brown wrapper. No strong, self-respecting Christian would want to be seen buying a book by this title—sort of like buying hemorrhoid medication at the drugstore! ("It's not for me!") But this is for you and for me.

Here is what I have learned as I have been forced to walk slowly:

"Even youths grow tired and weary, and young men stumble and fall; but those who hope in the LORD will renew their strength. They will soar on wings like eagles; they will run and not grow weary, they will walk and not be faint" (Isa. 40:30–31). This is God's promise to you, exhausted Christian! He sees you. He knows that look of exhaustion in your eyes. He has seen it many times before. "When my spirit grows faint within me," David prayed as he hid in a cave, "it is you who know my way" (Psalm 142:3).

God knows where you are. He has come to find you, to take your burden and give you back the joy of His saving help. I would like to share with you some things I've learned as I have walked this way with Him. There are wonderful things to learn. Take your time. We'll walk slowly. When we get tired, we'll sit for a while. The Lord of the harvest is patient to till and weed, plant and prune, feed and water, until He has nurtured from our overworked soil what is beautiful and pleasing to Him. Let us not grow weary, for the I AM who began this good work in us will carry it to completion (Phil. 1:6).

Karla Worley

CHAPTER 1

Come to Me, All Who Are Weary

*Come to me, all you who are weary and bur-
dened, and I will give you rest. Take my yoke
upon you and learn from me, for I am gentle
and humble in heart, and you will find rest for
your souls. For my yoke is easy and my burden
is light.*

—Matthew 11:28–30

*At the most unexpected moments in your life
there is this whisper of the Lord—"Come to
Me," and you are immediately drawn to Him.
Personal contact with Jesus changes everything.*

—Oswald Chambers[1]

A boy and his mother were waiting in
church for the worship service to begin. The boy was excited; this
was his first day to sit in the service! While watching all the people
coming and going, he noticed a large military plaque on the wall.
The plaque had many names listed on it.

"What is that, Mommy?" the boy asked.

"Oh, that," said his mother. "Those are the names of all the
people from our church who have died in the service."

"The 9:30 service or the 11:00 service?" the boy asked
anxiously.

I love this story. It reminds me of my own little boys, who each had a struggle with learning to sit through the worship service. When my youngest son, Ben, was four years old, it was his turn to graduate from extended session and come to "Big Church." On that first Sunday, I went to pick him up from Sunday School.

"Where are we going?" he asked.

"Today, you get to sit in Big Church," I answered.

We sat on the second row with his older brothers. The music began. The choir came in. Ben saw his daddy on the platform leading music. This was fun! We sang. Then we sat down.

"Now do I go back to my class?" Ben whispered.

"No, dear," I replied.

We prayed and read the Bible together. Someone sang a solo.

"Now do I go back to my class?" Ben asked again.

I shook my head. "Sh-sh!"

The pastor began to preach. Ben began to squirm.

"When do I go back to my class?" he asked.

"You don't," I whispered. "Now that you're a big boy, you sit through the whole service."

Ben responded loudly, "WELL, WHO SIGNED ME UP FOR THIS?"

If this is how you feel, here's a welcome invitation: "Come to me," Jesus beckons, "all you who are weary . . . . Take my yoke upon you and learn from me" (Matt. 11:28–29).

In the Jewish tradition of Jesus' time, there were many rabbis, each with his own interpretation of the Scriptures. Choosing to study under a particular rabbi, you became his *talmid* (disciple)— one who not only wanted to learn what his teacher knew, but who would imitate his lifestyle. This was called "taking the yoke" of the rabbi. (A "yoke" was an obligation or commitment.)

"Take my yoke upon you," Jesus invited His *talmidin* (disciples). "For my yoke is easy and my load is light." Though His life was far

2

from easy, Jesus walked with amazing lightness of heart, unencumbered by worry, unwounded by criticism, unfettered by greed or ambition, undeterred from His purpose. We can learn to live like that! Want to lighten your load? We must come to Him with the intent to learn and live as true disciples. Then, Jesus promised, "You will know the truth, and the truth will set you free" (John 8:32).

For years our church presented a "passion play" with angels, fishermen, Romans, and, of course, Pharisees. Although they did not sing, the Pharisees played an important part in the pageant. The Pharisees stood on the fringe of the crowds, murmuring disapprovingly, as if to say, "Whatever it is, we're against it!" (I'm sure you can imagine which of your church members would make good Pharisees.) Picture it: Jesus on the hillside, the crowd at His feet. Like other rabbis, He taught in parables; only His interpretation was very different. He spoke not of rule-keeping, but of a relationship. He corrected the wrong thinkers of the church— the Pharisees—who had made it hard to approach God (Matt. 23:1–13).

> So the Pharisees and teachers of the law asked Jesus, "Why don't your disciples live according to the tradition of the elders?"
>
> He replied, "Isaiah was right when he prophesied about you hypocrites; as it is written: 'These people honor me with their lips, but their hearts are far from me. They worship me in vain; their teachings are but rules taught by men'" (Mark 7:6–7).

You would think that after a lifetime of intense study of Scripture—teaching it, discussing it, memorizing it—the Pharisees would be the first to recognize and welcome Christ, but that wasn't the case. It hasn't worked for us, either. Oddly enough, one of the best places to avoid a relationship with God is to devote yourself to religion.

There is a difference.

Religious people pick nits. They major on technicalities. Their energies are spent on rituals, traditions, forms, procedures. They emphasize behavior. Relationship is about transformation of heart and character. Religion pronounces guilt. Relationship provides grace. Of all those Jesus confronted, He was hardest on the Pharisees. Why? Because they should have known better; and because, in trading relationship for religion, the Pharisees had misled and ensnared the flock with whom they were entrusted.

Jesus, seeing the crowd, "had compassion for them, because they were harassed and helpless, like sheep without a shepherd" (Matt. 9:36). If you know anything about sheep, you know they're stupid. Sheep couldn't find their way out of a paper bag. A shepherd on the Judean hillside would join other shepherds at night, building a stone wall around their sheep to protect them from wild animals. Encamped at the door of this "fold," they would take turns keeping watch. In the morning each shepherd would go to the door of the fold and call his flock. And here's the thing: Only the sheep belonging to that shepherd would leave the fold! As stupid as sheep are, there is one thing they know: their shepherd's voice.

The Bible continually uses the relationship of sheep to their shepherd to depict our relationship to God:

- Moses said to the LORD, "May the LORD . . . appoint a man over this community to go out and come in before them, one who will lead them out and bring them in, so the LORD's people will not be like sheep without a shepherd" (Num. 27:15–17).
- But he brought his people out like a flock; he led them like sheep through the desert (Psalm 78:52).

- Know that the LORD is God. It is he who made us, and we are his; we are his people, the sheep of his pasture (Psalm 100:3).
- I have strayed like a lost sheep. Seek your servant, for I have not forgotten your commands (Psalm 119:176).
- We all, like sheep, have gone astray, each of us has turned to his own way (Isa. 53:6).
- "You will all fall away," Jesus told them, "for it is written: I will strike the shepherd, and the sheep will be scattered" (Mark 14:27).
- For you were like sheep going astray, but now you have returned to the Shepherd and Overseer of your souls (1 Peter 2:25).

When God compares us to sheep, it's not a compliment. Real sheep are not those cute, fluffy creatures we see in the Hallmark store. Real sheep are smelly, dirty animals, and they are D-U-M . . . (uh) . . . B. That's the reality Jesus saw when He looked out on the crowds. That's the reality God foresaw the day He created the first of His flock, Adam and Eve. He knew we would all, like sheep, go astray, and that we would need a shepherd. Following the ways of the world and the ways of empty religion, we would become wearied and lose heart. Isaiah described this way of life: "Do and do, do and do, rule on rule, rule on rule; a little here, a little there" (Isa. 28:10).

Again, the original language makes me laugh. In the original Hebrew, it reads "*sav lasav sav lasav/kav lakav kav lakav,*"—a meaningless repetition of sounds, the Hebrew equivalent of "yada yada yada."[2] Sound like your way of life? Do and do, do and do . . . do-be-do-be-do.

God offers an alternative: "This is the resting place, let the weary rest" (Isa. 28:12). The word is *menuchah*, meaning "permanent resting place," the same word found in Isaiah 11:10: "Then it will come about in that day that the nations will resort to the root of Jesse . . . and His resting place will be glorious" (NASB). Jesus is the source of our promised rest. He is our permanent resting place (Heb. 4:7–10).

If you have become fatigued in producing what is pleasing to God, perhaps it is because you have been following the wrong shepherd.

- The man who enters by the gate is the shepherd of his sheep. The watchman opens the gate for him, and the sheep listen to his voice. He calls his own sheep by name and leads them out. When he has brought out all his own, he goes on ahead of them, and his sheep follow him because they know his voice. But they will never follow a stranger; in fact, they will run away from him because they do not recognize a stranger's voice (John 10:2–5).
- The thief comes only to steal and kill and destroy; I have come that they may have life, and have it to the full (John 10:10).
- I am the good shepherd; I know my sheep and my sheep know me (John 10:14).
- My sheep listen to my voice; I know them, and they follow me (John 10:27).

You were never meant to live a burdensome, tiresome life. The One we follow came to bring us abundant life—life to the fullest. *Thanks*, you're thinking, *my life is already crammed to overflowing*. Perhaps that's the problem. Our calendars are so full, we have no time for rest. Our checkbooks are so stretched, we cannot afford to rest. Our minds are noisy, our spirits depleted, our bodies exhausted. And our perspective has become so skewed, we actually take pride in this way of life. She who has the longest list wins.

🖋 My people have been lost sheep; their shepherds have led them astray and caused them to roam on the mountains. They wandered over mountain and hill and forgot their own resting place. Whoever found them devoured them (Jer. 50:6–7).

"My sheep listen to my voice . . . and they follow me," Jesus said. Let me ask you something: Can you even *hear* His voice over the noise of your life? Do you recognize it? Or have you mistaken another voice for His and been led astray into a life "crammed full"? Read again what Isaiah said: Whenever we wander from our resting place—Jesus—we become prey. Whoever finds us will devour us. School. Church. Work. Family. Media. They will eat away at our time, our values, our resources, our spirits, until they have devoured us. This breaks God's heart, for He loves us and longs to show compassion (Isa. 30:18). He pleads with us, "Hear, O my people, and I will speak" (Psalm 50:7).

That's Bible-lingo for what my mother used to say when I was not paying attention: "Now listen here, young lady . . ." Being a mother myself, I now understand how it concerns a parent when her child doesn't listen. "Today, if you hear his voice, do not harden your hearts," Hebrews 3:7–8 cautions. When Jesus calls us to Himself, and we recognize His voice, we have a choice: to obey or to stubbornly stay where we are. The writer of Hebrews cautions us not to make the same mistake the Israelites made when God called them to trust Him and enter the Promised Land. The author refers to this land as "the promised rest."

"So we see that they were not able to enter," Hebrews 3:19 states, "because of their unbelief."

The fact that you have opened this book and have read this far is evidence that you have heard Christ calling you to Himself. He has pursued you because He wants to remove the yoke of slavery you've adopted and give you His promised rest. God has gotten

7

personal with you. Don't make the mistake the Israelites did. "For we also have had the gospel preached to us, just as they did; but the message they heard was of no value to them, because those who heard did not combine it with faith" (Heb. 4:2). The faith referred to here is more than belief; it is hearing backed up by obedience. True, we have been set free from "have-to" religion. "But be careful to remember that you have been freed for one thing," warns Oswald Chambers, "to be absolutely devoted to your co-Worker,"[3] and to follow Him when He calls.

"Whenever the Spirit of God breaks into our lives," writes Brennan Manning in *The Signature of Jesus*, "in the middle of the day, in the middle of the week, or the middle of a lifetime, it is to announce in some fashion that the time for pussyfooting is over."[4] For a long time before I crashed, I knew that my lifestyle was out of control. I knew that the stress, anxiety, weariness, and constant have-tos that drove me were not anything I recognized in the life of Christ. With a growing uneasiness, I heard His voice correcting me, but I looked around at my fellow Christians, both lay and professional, and saw that they were just as exhausted, just as busy. They seemed to be keeping up, and I didn't want to appear to be a wimp.

Here is where I made a serious mistake. Jesus' invitation is "Come to *me*, and *I* will give you rest." The church will not give you rest. All the Bible-study groups you can join will not give you rest. All the conferences and retreats you may attend will not give you rest. Only Jesus is Rest. You cannot lighten your load by coming to meetings *about* Him. You must come to Him personally.

In Jesus' time, a *talmid* would sit at his rabbi's feet as the rabbi interpreted the Torah. The talmid learned firsthand from his teacher. This is how Jesus describes His relationship with those who come to Him. Jesus will teach us firsthand what pleases His father. "Take my yoke upon you," is His invitation, and it is a personal one. He Himself will be our teacher. "It is written in the Prophets: 'They will all be taught by God,'" Jesus said. "Everyone who listens to the Father and learns from him comes to me" (John 6:45).

Jesus modeled this relationship in His own earthly life: "But Jesus often withdrew to lonely places and prayed" (Luke 5:16). There was no one else on earth with whom Jesus could talk Spirit-to-Spirit. Jesus had to get One-on-One with His Father.

"The key words for our consideration are . . . *but*, and *often* . . . . *But* indicates an effort exerted against the pervading pressures," writes Jean Fleming in *Living the Christ-centered Life Between Walden and the Whirlwind*. "Jesus didn't subject Himself to the whims of man. He didn't just flow with the tide. Unlike a leaf carried along by the water, Jesus made choices. Despite the opportunities for service, He chose to withdraw. *Often* indicates habit, custom, pattern. Jesus *often* withdrew to pray."[5]

I must confess that I most often turn to anyone and everyone else before I turn to God. I can recall times of frustration when I needed comfort or counsel, and all I got were busy signals and answering machines. Imagine God's sadness as I ignored His invitation, "Come to me." (A former pastor once said, "If you ever go to a friend with a problem, and he or she does not immediately say, 'Let's go to Jesus,' don't ever turn to that friend for counsel again. That person is not wise.")

I do remember a recent time when I did turn to God instead to others. As usual during the past year, I was tired. Tired of daily life. Tired of coping with illness. Tired of keeping up with work. Just tired of being tired. I got in my car and drove to a nearby park with a small lake that is like a sanctuary to me. I parked and walked way back into the woods, to a rude platform that serves as a kind of small pier by the edge of the lake. I can't explain it, but I felt almost driven to be at that spot; I knew God would meet me there. I desperately needed to be with Jesus, and I clearly heard Him saying, "Come to me, you who are weary."

I didn't say anything. I didn't hear anything. I just leaned against a tree while the wind rustled the leaves and blew through my hair. When I was a little girl and needed comforting, my mother would sit beside me and stroke my hair—not saying anything, just stroking. That's how the wind felt to me that day—like the hand of God, silent and comforting.

"The LORD is *my* shepherd," wrote David. "*He* restores my soul" (Psalm 23:1, 3; italics mine). My friend Debra Berry recalls when she and her cousins would gather around their grandmother and each would lay claim to her: "She is *my* grandmother." "No, she's *my* grandmother." This touches the core of faith: ". . . to believe in a personal God who calls me and leads me," writes Manning.[6] But the Bible assures us that God Himself goes out of His way to find each lost sheep. He will not rest while even one of us is in danger.

> For this is what the Sovereign LORD says: I myself will search for my sheep and look after them. As a shepherd looks after his scattered flock when he is with them, so will I look after my sheep. I will rescue them from all the places where they were scattered (Ezek. 34:11–12).

Jesus explained it this way: "Suppose one of you has a hundred sheep and loses one of them. Does he not leave the ninety-nine in the open country and go after the lost sheep until he finds it? And when he finds it, he joyfully puts it on his shoulders and goes home" (Luke 15:4–6). Notice something: the shepherd *joyfully* rescues the sheep, and when he does, he carries the sheep on his own shoulders. God wants to break the bars of the heavy yoke of obligation you have taken and replace it with His yoke, which is not burdensome. He *wants* to rescue you from the hands of those who have enslaved you. It is His pleasure to do that. He does not come trudging after us, muttering, "When I find you, you're in for it!"

He pursues us because He loves us.

And if the shepherd is joyful to find the sheep, can you imagine how glad the sheep is to be found?

The first summer our family vacationed at the beach retreat where we spend a week each year, our son Ben was just learning to ride a bike. He was so carried away with the power of his new wheels that he often zoomed down the bike path ahead of us, undeterred by the fact that he had no idea where he was going. One morning as he and I were returning to the house, Ben took a detour off the bike path that led him into unfamiliar woods. I could hear him through the trees, crying. Although he was only a few yards away, he could not see me, but he could hear me.

"Ben!" I cried, "Where are you?"

"Mommy!" he called back. "I'm lost! Find me, Mommy!"

For the next few terrifying moments, I called "Ben!" repeatedly, while he called "Mommy!" I tried to find my way toward the sound of his voice, like some bizarre version of the "Marco Polo" water game. When I found him he rushed into my arms, trembling. He was so glad to be found.

Jesus described this kind of childlike gladness in Mark 10:15: "I tell you the truth," He said, "anyone who will not receive the kingdom of God like a little child will never enter it." Glad to be found. Glad to be taught. Just glad to be in His presence.

When our oldest son Seth was a child, we loved to watch him discover new things every day.

"Yook, Mommy!" he would say with his funny toddler pronunciation. "Yook, Daddy!" he would exclaim, pointing to something wondrous he had just seen.

Christ invites us to come to Him and discover a new way of life, and this is the picture He paints. When we take His yoke, it is not burdensome, because every day is filled with joyous, wonderful discoveries.

"See," God declares in Isaiah 43:19, "I am doing a new thing!"

Imagine His disappointment when our response is fear or boredom—or worse, when we don't even stop to look at what He is showing us. Imagine His delight when we exclaim, "Look, Daddy! I see it!"

That's what David understood when he sang, "You have made known to me the path of life; you will fill me with joy in your presence" (Psalm 16:11).

Adam and Eve knew this joy. In the cool of the day, Genesis 3 tells us, God would come and walk with them in the garden. Perhaps they would walk in the companionable silence of those who know each other well. Perhaps they would run to Him the moment He came into view, as my son Matt still does each afternoon, bursting with tales of new things discovered that day. Perhaps they would sit by the lake, and He would stroke their hair. But that was before the serpent deceived them and destroyed their perfect fellowship with God.

Did you know that the weariness of hard labor, which produces little, is a result of the fall of man? (See Genesis 3:17–19.) The work that God gave us to do was to be fruitful and to enjoy His harvest and His presence. The moment the shame of sin broke their perfect union of fellowship, God's first act was to go looking for man, calling, "Where are you?" He then began calling us back to Himself.

This is what the whole Bible is about! God *wants* His people to experience the life He intended for them, the abundant life—not the exhausted servitude into which we have wandered. He wants you back—even more than you want out. And He has made a way, carrying you on His own shoulders. The same way we receive salvation is the way we are rescued from slavery: Jesus Christ.

Our first step toward a life free of weariness is to turn away from our burdens. Now I invite you to take the second step: Turn toward Christ. Listen for His voice. Your Good Shepherd is compassionately, joyfully calling you: "Come to me."

CHAPTER 2

Consider Him, So That You Do Not Grow Weary

Consider him who endured such opposition from sinful men, so that you will not grow weary and lose heart.

—Hebrews 12:3

To me, "I am the way" is a better statement than "I know the way."

—Thich Nhat Hanh[1]

*M*y children are into the "What Would Jesus Do?" merchandise—T-shirts, armbands, shoestrings. The other day my youngest sons had a knock-down, drag-out fight over who would wear the red WWJD bracelet to school. One thing I know Jesus would NOT do: Jesus would not punch out his little brother just so He could wear the red WWJD bracelet!

The problem with asking "What would Jesus do?" is that it's easy for us to determine what we think Jesus would do, and then go do it—bypassing Him altogether in the process. For instance, just an hour ago I was thinking that if Jesus were working as hard as I am on a book manuscript, He would surely eat at least half a package of chocolate chip cookies. Now I'm joking, but we undertake some equally absurd things on God's behalf.

The Apostle Paul, describing his life before he met Christ, said he was convinced that there were many things he was doing for God (Acts 26:9). Those "things" were persecuting and martyring the new followers of Christ! This is what can happen when we attempt to do God's work our way. World history, your personal history, and my personal history are strewn with sad examples. Jesus does not need me to think up what to do for Him; He needs me to allow Him to live in me. I have a new set of armbands for everyone to wear: JLJD (Just Let Jesus Do It!).

The writer of Hebrews encouraged believers to run with perseverance the race set before them and prescribed the antidote for growing weary: "Let us *fix our eyes on Jesus*, the author and perfecter of our faith, who for the joy set before him endured the cross, scorning its shame, and sat down at the right hand of the throne of God. *Consider him* who endured such opposition from sinful men, *so that you will not grow weary and lose heart*" (Heb. 12:2–3, italics mine).

When the author of Hebrews used the phrase "fix our eyes" in his original language, he was saying, "Let us look away from all else, and look only to Jesus." We tend to fix our eyes on the details of life rather than on the Source of life. We ask God for a "To do" list, not the presence of the One who made this day. We seek peace instead of the One who is our Peace. We pray for guidance, when we have the Guide. Why? Haven't we proven that nothing else will satisfy?

Maintaining a code of behavior exhausts us. Inspiration grows thin. Motivation by a charismatic leader is temporary. Pursuing approbation wearies us. Religious rituals become tedious. All methods (or yokes) will be burdensome except following Christ, fixing our eyes on Him and living His lifestyle. "It is a stunning New Testament truth," writes John Piper in *Let the Nations Be Glad*, "that since the incarnation of the Son of God all saving faith must henceforth fix on him."[2] Let us look away from all else.

"Consider Him," urged the writer of Hebrews, "so that you will not grow weary and lose heart." The word *consider* comes from two Greek roots: *logizomai*, which means to "reckon" or "take into account," and *ana*, which means "again" or "back." The writer knows that our gaze will wander away from Christ, so he urges us to go back again and again and factor Him in. I find it interesting that neither Greek phrase—"turn away from all else" nor "go back again and factor Him in"—is used anywhere else in the New Testament. Not once. They are solely applied to Jesus, specifically to following Him without growing weary.

Our response as disciples is not to a call, a calling, a work, or a set of beliefs or practices. Our response is to a person: Jesus Christ. Anything else but Christ becomes a burden. Anything less than the pursuit of the person of Jesus Christ—to know Him and become like Him—is a poor substitute. We cannot settle for the ritual of religion. We cannot stand on the credentials of churchmanship. We cannot look to good works or duty. We cannot rely on warm feelings. We cannot trust in a hand-me-down faith. Brennan Manning describes his own experience of entering into a personal relationship with Christ:

> After twenty-two years of living by second-hand faith, on February 8, 1956, I met Jesus and moved . . . from belief to faith. It was noon. The Angelus bell from a cloistered Carmelite monastery sounded in the distance. I was kneeling in a small chapel in Loretto, Pennsylvania. At five minutes after three, I rose shakily from the floor knowing that the greatest adventure of my life had just begun. I entered a new perspective accurately described by Paul in Colossians 3:11: "Christ is all, and is in all."
>
> During those three hours on my knees, I felt like a little boy kneeling at the seashore. Little waves

washed up and lapped against my knees. Slowly the waves grew bigger and stronger until they reached my waist. Suddenly a tremendous wave of concussion force knocked me over backward and swept me off the beach reeling in midair, arching through space, vaguely aware that I was being carried to a place I had never been before—the heart of Jesus Christ . . . until, without warning, a hand gripped my heart. I could barely breathe. . . . The love of Christ, the crucified Son of God, took on the wildness, fury, and passion of a sudden spring storm. Jesus died on the cross for me!

I had known that before . . . . But in one blinding moment of salvific truth it was real knowledge calling for personal engagement of my mind and heart. Christianity was being loved and falling in love with Jesus Christ. Later the words in the first letter of Peter would illuminate and verify my experience: "You did not see him, yet you love him; and still without seeing him, you are already filled with a joy so glorious that it cannot be described, because you believe; and you are sure of the end to which your faith looks forward, that is, the salvation of your soul" (1:8–9).[3]

Can you say that you have had a personal encounter with Jesus Christ?

This is what kept the Apostle Paul going in the midst of discouraging, life-threatening times. It wasn't his concern for the new believers or his commitment to sound doctrine. It was his love for the person Jesus Christ that compelled Paul to press on and not give up or grow weary. "I consider everything a loss compared to the surpassing greatness of knowing Christ Jesus my Lord," wrote Paul. "But one thing I do: Forgetting what is behind and straining toward what is ahead, I press on" (Phil. 3:8, 13–14). What inspired this single-minded passion? Paul had met Christ face-to-face. (See Acts 9 and 1 Corinthians 9:1.)

This was the distinguishing credential of the New Testament apostles, what set them apart from the other believers: they were eyewitnesses to Christ. "God has raised this Jesus to life, and we are all witnesses of the fact," Peter proclaimed (Acts 2:32). "The Word became flesh and blood, and moved into the neighborhood," wrote John. "We saw the glory with our own eyes" (John 1:14, *The Message*). This firsthand knowledge was crucial to their perseverance. Jesus was not an abstract concept to these men: He was real. They saw the flesh and they saw the blood. Their friendship with Him was personal. They were not motivated by the idea of Jesus; they were compelled by Jesus Himself.

It is no coincidence that these men risked everything for Christ, devoting the rest of their lives to bring others face-to-face with Him by faith. With indefatigable passion, they birthed the church in Judea, Scythia, Greece, Armenia, Palestine, Egypt, Asia Minor, Syria, Persia, India, Africa, Central Asia, Italy, Sicily, and Macedonia. They penned twenty-four of the twenty-seven books of the New Testament, including the firsthand, eyewitness accounts of Matthew, John, Peter, and Paul. Without exception, every one of them was martyred for his faith in Jesus Christ. In the face of flogging, torture, imprisonment, deprivation, and death they could not stop talking about what they had seen and heard. (See Acts 4.)

What explains their complete abandonment to Christ, when His followers today have a hard time mustering up the energy to get up for church on Sunday morning? Do we not know the same Jesus?

Perhaps not.

Let me ask you: how well do you know Jesus?

When I posed this question to my friends, I was shocked to discover that eight out of ten could not say they had ever really had a firsthand encounter with Christ. They know about Him and believe in Him, but don't feel that they have ever experienced His presence or heard Him speak to them personally. These are Bible-Belt-bred, churchgoing women who serve and lead faithfully in their local congregations!

No wonder we are running on empty!

Hear me say this: I believe in missions, in ministry, and in service. But service undertaken apart from the person of Jesus Christ is nothing more than Peace Corps. And sooner or later, you will get tired of that.

We do not serve a cause. We are not committed to an ideology. We have not been called to a good work. We have been called to the heart of a person—the living Christ. He is as much alive and real today as He was when He inhabited human flesh. He speaks. He listens. He prays. He appoints. And He empowers. We must know Him firsthand, because apart from Him we can do nothing (John 15:5).

Manning writes, "Each one of us bears the responsibility of responding to the call of Christ individually and committing ourselves to him personally. Do I believe in Jesus or in the preachers, teachers, and cloud of witnesses who have spoken to me about him? Is the Christ of my belief really my own or that of theologians, pastors, parents, and Oswald Chambers? . . . His question to Peter: Who do you say that I am? is addressed to every would-be disciple."[4]

My pastor, Mike Glenn, has brought this question to life for me as he imagines what will one day happen around the throne in heaven. It will be testimony time. Moses will get up and tell his story. Elijah will tell his. David will sing a favorite psalm. Daniel will recall the long night in the lion's den. John the Baptist will nod his head. (He will have his head then!) Mary will show Jesus' baby pictures. James will complain about having the perfect kid for a brother. Paul and Peter will remember the first believers and the terrible persecutions. Luke will describe the miracles, and John will recount what it was like to lean at His side. There will be hundreds of others who knew Him and walked with Him—by faith if not by sight: Martin Luther, John Wesley, Fanny Crosby, Keith Green, Jim Elliot, Cassie Bernall. And then they will turn to you.

"Tell us your story," they will ask. "How do you know Him?" And what will you say?

"God is our refuge and strength, an ever-present help in trouble," the sons of Korah proclaimed. "Therefore we will not fear, though the earth give way and the mountains fall into the heart of the sea" (Psalm 46:1–2). This was their personal testimony. They had seen the earth give way.

The sons of Korah were descendants of the Kohathite branch of Levites, those responsible for transporting the sacred articles of the Holy of Holies. Only members of Aaron's priestly line were allowed to enter this sacred place where God dwelt. God warned the Kohathites not to even look upon the sacred things or they would die. Korah led a rebellion against Moses and Aaron, disregarding God's instruction and arguing that his family was just as qualified to approach God as Aaron's. God destroyed Korah and his followers. They, their families, and everything they owned were swallowed into the ground as the other tribes watched. But in His mercy, God spared a remnant of the sons of Korah, who later became leaders of worship in the temple. Their psalms reflect their gratitude for having been allowed to live although they had challenged God's authority. "He lifts his voice, the earth melts," they sang. "The Lord Almighty is with us." Notice what they called Him: "The God of Jacob is our fortress" (Psalm 46:7). Jacob, too, wrestled with God and survived (Gen. 32).

"Those who know your name will trust in you," the psalmist proclaimed (Psalm 9:10). Do you know Him as Provider? Then you will trust Him with your needs. Do you know Him as Lord? Then you will trust Him with your choices. Do you know Him as the Truth? Then you will trust Him when you do not understand.

The name by which we know Him reveals our relationship to Him. The Pharisees called Him "Teacher," but the disciples called Him "Master." They abandoned everything and bound their lives to Him, twenty-four hours a day, seven days a week. So when Peter declared, "You are the Son of the living God," Jesus answered, "Blessed are you . . . for this was not revealed to you by man, but by my Father in heaven" (Matt. 16:16–17).

Years ago I came across a comprehensive list of the names for God used in the Bible.[5] I keep this list stuck in my prayer journal. I have turned to it many times. When I am so overwhelmed by a situation that I don't even know how to pray about it, I run down this list and speak those names by which I need to know Him: Sanctuary, He who comforts you, He who reveals His thoughts to man, the God who sees me, my Defender. This is what we mean when we say, "lift up His name." Just hold it out there. His name is His covenant with you; He has pledged to honor it. The by-product of praying this way is that I have learned something crucial to perseverance: I must get my attention off the situation and fix it instead upon the One who is greater than my circumstance and who is with me in the midst of it. It is more important that I know Him than that I know what to do.

So I ask you again: How well do you know Jesus? Do you know Him by a personal name? Do you have a history with Him? Are the markers of His presence along the pathway in your life?

In the Old Testament, when a person encountered God face-to-face it was customary to mark the spot with an altar, usually a pile of stones. This marker would serve two purposes: It would serve as a reminder to you and as a witness to others that God indeed gets personal. Samuel called his altar of stone "Ebenezer," which meant, "So far the Lord has helped us" (1 Sam. 7:12). Jacob called the place "Peniel" where he wrestled all night with God "because I saw God face to face, and yet my life was spared" (Gen. 32:30). Forever those markers stood as testimony of those who knew God personally.

"Look to the LORD and his strength; seek his face always. Remember the wonders he has done," exhorts the psalmist (105:4–5). Keep a record of your history with God—the names by which you know Him, the wonders He has done, the answers He has given to your prayers. When you grow weary, your "history book" will be a source of encouragement. When you doubt, you can look back and say, "I was there."

"Being saved and seeing Jesus are not the same thing," wrote Oswald Chambers. "Many people who have never seen Jesus have received and are in God's grace. But once you have seen Him, you can never be the same."[6]

How well do you want to know Christ?

It will cost you. Jacob forever walked with a limp. Zacchaeus went out on a limb—literally. It could cost you your life, as it has cost many believers, even in parts of the world today. Certainly it will cost you some of your preconceived notions about who He is and what He expects. You will have to give up your busyness in order to get to know Him. Are you willing to do less in order to know Him more? You will have to sit at His feet. You will have to obey Him, and come to know Him by walking with Him. You will need to spend time listening to Him and studying His Word, taking on His mind. You will have to revise your values. You will be required to surrender your pride and your self-reliance, trusting yourself to His strength and His ways.

When Jesus said, "I am the way," He was not speaking to the unwashed masses of people we would consider lost; He was speaking intimately with His inner circle of disciples at the last Passover meal (John 14). He was breaking the news of His impending persecution and death—and their own, which would follow shortly.

> Do not let your hearts be troubled. Trust in God; trust also in me," [Jesus told them]. "You know the way to the place where I am going."

Thomas said to him, "Lord, we don't know where you are going, so how can we know the way?"

Jesus answered, "I am the way . . . ."

Philip said, "Lord, show us the Father and that will be enough for us."

Jesus answered: "Don't you know me, Philip, even after I have been among you such a long time? Anyone who has seen me has seen the Father. How can you say, 'Show us the Father'?" (John 14:1–9).

It breaks my heart to hear the pain that catches in Jesus' throat when He says, "Don't you know me?" But I know from personal experience that it is possible to be so busy for Jesus that you hardly pay any attention to Him at all. I know it is possible to spend years in His presence and still not recognize Him. To know Him takes intense personal pursuit of Jesus Christ above everything else. We know Jesus as well as we choose to know Him. It is much easier for us to *do for* Him than to *be with* Him. We run to activity every time, because it is tangible, something we can check off our list. "Jesus is the hardest part of the religion to grasp, to keep alive," a Jesuit monk once confessed.[7] But He is most worth it. To bypass Him on the busy road of life is to lose our way. And many of us— pillars of the church—are utterly lost.

The Apostle Paul put it succinctly: "To live is Christ" (Phil. 1:21). Everything else—everything—is no life at all.

CHAPTER 3

Growing Weary in Worship

Be still, and know that I am God; I will be exalted among the nations, I will be exalted in the earth.

—Psalm 46:10

When wonder is dead, the soul is a dry bone.
—Bishop William Quayle[1]

A kindergarten teacher gave her class a show-and-tell assignment: bring something to represent your family's religion. On show-and-tell day, each child stood to make his or her presentation.

The first little boy said, "My name is Tommy and I am Catholic, and this is a crucifix." The second little boy said, "My name is Benjamin and I am Jewish, and this is the Star of David." The third little boy said, "My name is Billy and I am a Baptist, and this is a casserole."

Let's face it, when you and I are called to demonstrate our faith, we most often whip out our "To do" lists.

Q: How many churchwomen does it take to change a light bulb?
A: One to change the light bulb, four to decorate, two to get the door prizes, and three to bring the chicken salad.

On my husband's desk is a sign that reads, "Jesus is coming! Look busy!" Dennis is a consummate list-maker; but he's learned that being busy for God is not the same as being present with God. Churches are full of people so busy in the kitchen, on the committee, or in the choir that they never actually sit down with God. Jesus is coming; there is work to be done and Christ commissioned us to do it, but not at the expense of the opportunity to sit down with Him right here, right now, face-to-face and first—above all else.

In several of the churches where I have visited, I have noticed a sign posted over the door of the sanctuary: Enter to Worship— Depart to Serve. I say "Amen!" to that. There has been a lot of focus on worship in the past few years. Some denominations dismiss it as a fad. One church leader I know calls it "stand and sway"— just a bunch of people striving to "feel good" about Jesus.

"It never leads anywhere past that," he complains. "It's *all about me.*" He thinks we just need to return to the good old missions hymns and revival preaching. (Some of you will say "Amen!" to this.)

Yes, worship without service is "all about me." It is too introspective and does not accurately reflect the heart of Christ. But let me hasten to say that service without worship is also "all about me," because it is rooted in self-motivation and a sense of obligation. We need both worship and service. Worship overflows into service, which in turn responds with worship—a continually renewing cycle. Apart from worship, service becomes a duty and a burden. "Missions is not the ultimate goal of the church," writes John Piper. "Worship is."[2]

I sat in the audience of a large denominational missions meeting where my friend Sherri quoted John Piper's words. You could hear the air being sucked out of the room by the collective gasp her opening statement garnered. I had to laugh. Only passionate, intense Sherri would have the courage to make that bold and shocking statement to such a group of people! She also has had the courage to plant her life (which includes three children under the age of three) halfway around the world among one of the last people groups to hear the gospel of Jesus Christ. Duty did not motivate her to do this. She is driven by her passion for Christ, by who she knows Him to be, and she has rearranged her life to see that others know Him, too.

Don't misunderstand me. Worship is not a pep rally to pump us up so that we can go out and win one for the Big Guy. The function of worship is not to dazzle us into offering Christ our lives, to give us spiritual goose bumps. The point of worship is not "Ah!" but "Aha!" In worship our eyes are opened to see God, to see ourselves, and to see our world from God's point of view. Lillian Hellman explains: "Old paint on canvas, as it ages, sometimes becomes transparent. When that happens it is possible, in some pictures, to see the original lines: a tree will show through a woman's dress, a child makes way for a dog, a large boat is no longer on an open sea. That is called *pentimento* because the painter "repented," changed his mind. Perhaps it would be as well to say that the old conception, replaced by a later choice, is a way of seeing and then seeing again."[3]

A way of seeing and then seeing again—this is the effect of worship. Coming before the Almighty, we realize our place in the grand scheme, we repent of our old conceptions, and we receive a new vision.

This is exactly what happened to the prophet Isaiah. "In the year that King Uzziah died," Isaiah related, "I saw the Lord" (Isa. 6:1). Beth Moore points out that Isaiah's reference to Uzziah is significant, because until now King Uzziah was Isaiah's definition of greatness and power.[4] But in the year Uzziah died, Isaiah was able to see real glory.

When we do not worship, we grow weary in doing good. But worship reminds us who God is. "Be still, and know that I am God," (Psalm 46:10). God might add, "And *you* are not!" My Dad likes to say, "That's why your name is spelled K-A-R-L-A and not G-O-D." No kidding. And we can thank our lucky stars that *I* am not God, because you'd be in big trouble right now. But sometimes I act like I'm in charge, as though it's all up to me. That's when I start to grow very weary . . . and also whiny.

It's comforting to know that even great prophets like Isaiah and his predecessor Elijah had whiny moments. (See Elijah's story in 1 Kings 18–19.) After the spiritual high of Mount Carmel, Elijah fled for his life from an angry Jezebel. These events drained him, physically and spiritually. Elijah was worn out. After all his hard work on God's behalf, things hadn't turned out as he'd hoped. He felt sorry for himself. In effect, he prayed, "I want to die."

There are some prayers to which God answers, "I'm going to pretend I didn't hear that." Aren't you glad? This is one of those times. God let Elijah cry himself to sleep; He didn't even try to argue. Elijah was so tired, he wouldn't have heard a word God said anyway. Have you ever felt like that? Ever come away from a worship service or Bible study, having sat through it like a stone, only to have someone say, "That was the greatest blessing"? We can become so physically and spiritually weary that we are too tired to hear.

Many of us are too foolish to lie down and rest. My pastor, Mike Glenn, says that when he reads Psalm 23, what jumps out is the phrase, "He *makes me* lie down in green pastures." He has to *make* me lie down, like a parent with a too-tired child.

When my son Seth was a baby, he did not like to go to bed. He would cry and cry. Being a first-time mother, it was excruciating for me to endure what seemed like hours of his protests (though it was actually only about ten minutes). "Be firm," said my pediatrician, "Don't give in." Seth would stand up in his crib, cling to the side, and wail at the top of his lungs. Then suddenly—clunk—he would fall over asleep in mid-howl.

Apparently this is what Elijah did. He threw himself under a broom tree and wailed until he passed out. And do you know what he cried? "I am the only one left. Nobody else cares about You, God. It's all up to me." Ever feel like that? "If I don't keep teaching this class, or chairing this committee, or making this event happen, it'll just dry up and blow away. Nobody cares but me." Uh-huh. Been there.

A country church got itself a new preacher, who everybody thought was terrific until he started a weird habit. Every Monday he would go down to the train station and sit on the bench to wait for a train to arrive. As the train came into view, the preacher would leap to his feet, jump up and down, and cheer as the train approached. The passengers would disembark, new passengers would get on, and as the train pulled away from the station, the preacher would cheer it on until it was out of sight.

After a few weeks of this, the deacons got worried, so they went to see the man.

"Ah, preacher," they said, "we've been hearing some mighty strange stories about you."

"Oh, you mean the train thing?" said the preacher. He sighed. "I love that train. It's the only thing moving in this town that I don't have to get behind and shove."

It's a sure symptom that we have grown weary in doing good when we start thinking it's all up to us. There is a hilarious passage in Isaiah 26 that addresses this. (You may not think of Isaiah as a hilarious book, but stay with me.) "LORD, *you* establish peace for us; all that we have accomplished *you* have done for us. As a woman with child and about to give birth writhes and cries out in her pain, so were we in your presence, O LORD. We were with child, we writhed in pain, but we gave birth to wind. *We* have not brought salvation to the earth; *we* have not given birth to people of the world" (Isa. 26:12, 17–18, italics mine).

I laugh when I read this because it reminds me of my first pregnancy. Although I was only about eight weeks along, my stomach already stuck out and my clothes didn't fit because I had intense and terribly uncomfortable gas. It felt like I was sitting on a knife blade, the gas pains were so intense. If you'd stuck me with a pin,

I would surely have blown out the window like a big balloon. "We writhed in pain, like a woman about to give birth," described Isaiah; and so did I—only nothing came out but, well, wind!

We can expend enormous effort with the best intentions, but human effort will never produce heaven's results. When you are gone, your efforts will blow away like the wind. "Flesh gives birth to flesh," Jesus explained, "but the Spirit gives birth to spirit" (John 3:6). We will never give birth to the peoples of the world; only God can. When we grow weary we tend to forget who is God and who isn't.

After Elijah had a long nap, God woke him and said, "The journey is too much for you" (1 Kings 19:7).

Psalm 131 has come to mean a lot to me. It is a brief little psalm that, paraphrased, says, "I have quieted my heart. I have not concerned myself with things too great for me." Here is what I am learning: Everything is too great for me. I don't need to try to run any of it. I am sure that sometimes Jesus surveys my situation and says to me what He said to His disciples: "The harvest is plentiful, but the workers are few. Ask the Lord of the harvest, therefore, to send out workers into his harvest field" (Luke 10:2). Jesus knew His disciples' limitations very well. Looking out on the enormity of the task, He advised, "You boys had better pray for back-up. You're not up to this."

"I lift up my eyes to the hills—where does my help come from? My help comes from the LORD, the Maker of heaven and earth" (Psalm 121:1–2). Psalms 120 through 134 are called the "Songs of Ascent." Each spring all Jewish males would journey to Jerusalem for the Passover Feast. As they traveled they would sing songs of faith. Climbing to the temple mount, the pilgrims could look up at the surrounding hillsides to see temples to pagan gods. "Where does our help come from?" they sang. "From the Great I AM, the One true God who made heaven and earth."

At least once a year I make my own journey—to the beach. It's a long trip, but entirely worth it the moment I stand at the edge of the

Atlantic Ocean. It's good for the soul to be confronted with the vastness of creation. If you can't get to the beach, a mountain or tree will do. Or go outside to look up into the night sky. We lose our perspective in a man-made world. On a recent beach trip, I read Isaiah 66:1–2: "Heaven is My throne and the earth is My footstool. Where then is a house you could build for Me? And where is a place that I may rest? For My hand made all these things" (NASB).

"My ways are different from yours" (Isa. 55:8 TEV), says the Lord. We are all weary from trying to accomplish His work our way. It's exhausting being God. That's because He is, and we're not. Be still long enough, and you will know that.

The Jews observed (and still practice) the custom of the Sabbath, a day of rest and worship following every six days of labor (Ex. 31:12–17). The Hebrew word *shabbath* means to stop or rest regularly as a ritual or observance. God established the observance of Sabbath as a sign of His unique relationship with His chosen people. God's intent for Sabbath was "so you may know that I am the LORD, who makes you holy" (v. 13). When God's people fail to observe Sabbath rest, it is a sign we have forgotten who He is. When we do not worship, we do not rest.

The practice of Sabbath extended beyond the seventh day to the seventh month, the seventh year; it applied to the performance of household duties, farming, business, and the life of the community. Sabbath was built into the rhythm of life. By keeping Sabbath, then and now, God's people acknowledge that we know who is the Lord of all of these things—and who is not. By obeying these instructions, the Israelites said to the world, "Our Father knows best." When they flourished while others famished, the cultures around them took notice and said, "Their God must be right." The blessings of this obedience are enumerated in Leviticus 26; as are the inevitable results of disobedience (Lev. 26:33–35).

What happens when we neglect God's Sabbaths? Our spiritual, emotional, and material resources become overworked, worn out, dried up. Our collapse, Isaiah prophesied, is like "pieces of pottery, shattered so mercilessly that among its pieces not a fragment will be found" (Isa. 30:14). We are useless as vessels for God's glory. If God's people are as overworked, overcommitted, overweight, and overspent as the world around us, who is going to take notice of us and say, "Their God must be right"?

"The fear of the LORD leads to life; then one rests content, untouched by trouble" (Prov. 19:23). Conversely, forgetting our place and usurping God's leads to death, to lack of rest, to never being satisfied. A heart that does not worship meets the day under-supplied, thirsty, lonely, unwise, and joyless. But "the fear of the LORD is a fountain of life" (Prov. 14:27).

Also, "the fear of the LORD is the beginning of knowledge" (Prov. 1:7). What is the fear of the Lord? It is knowing who God is and who we are. It is realizing our place. It is the perspective that prompts us to bow down and humble ourselves before the all-knowing, all-wise God. It is what causes us to worship. Because when we see God as He truly is, we see ourselves as we truly are.

"Where were you when I laid the earth's foundation?" God thundered to Job. "Who marked off its dimensions? Surely you know! . . . Who shut up the sea behind doors? . . . Have you ever given orders to the morning? . . . or walked in the recesses of the deep?" (Job 38:4–16).

Well . . . no.

Job's response was to shut his mouth.

"Oh," he said, like a big-mouthed frog.

Isaiah shuffled into the temple mourning the loss of Uzziah. But when he came face-to-face with God, he cried, "Woe is me!" He, too, saw something new: "I am a man of unclean lips."

Just imagine what might happen next Sunday if the church members—so busy slamming car doors, dragging children, and straightening hair-bows and neckties—came face-to-face with God and stopped in mid-aisle to confess.

"I cheated on my taxes!"

"I yelled at my kids!"

"I pinched my brother!"

"I didn't want to come!"

That would be an unforgettable service (and a long one!).

We are uncomfortable with confession. *That's* an understatement. In fact, we are petrified at the thought. So we have removed it from our liturgies and put enough distance between us and our fellow believers that we can fool them with appearances. We appear to have learned how to walk and talk, how to dress and behave. We know the "stand up" and "sit down" chords. We line up well-scrubbed in our pews. We stand up and sit down in all the correct places. And no one ever dares raise his or her hand to say, "Excuse me, this is *hard* for me! Is it hard for you? Am I the *only one* having trouble here?"

An Amish boy and his father went into a shopping mall, where they saw a sight they had never seen before: a set of shiny silver walls that moved apart and went back together. People were going in and out through these walls.

"What is this, Father?" asked the boy.

"I do not know, Son," replied the father. "Let's watch."

As they watched, a shriveled old woman painfully steered her wheelchair up to the set of silver walls and pushed the button. The walls moved apart and the old woman slowly wheeled herself into the tiny room beyond. Then the shiny walls closed, and flashing lights went off above them. Finally they opened and a beautiful teenage girl walked out! The father turned to his son and said, "Go get your mother!"

Don't you wish you had a set of those shiny silver walls in your church? You could shove people through them, and they would come out perfect—no problems, complaints, or opinions that irritate you. Wouldn't that be great? So far, I haven't found any church that has a set of those walls.

But here's the thing: we act like we do. We don't mean to, but here's how it happens: I was sitting in a Vacation Bible School opening assembly one morning when a woman from my church shared her testimony with the children. "I was six years old when I became a Christian," she said. "It was on a Sunday. The pastor had talked about sin that day. When I went home, I asked my mother, 'What is sin?' And she said, 'Sin is all the bad things we do. The bad things we do build a wall between us and God's love. But God loves us so much, He sent His Son Jesus to die on the cross to break down that wall. And when we become Christians, Jesus comes to live in our hearts, and He takes away our sin.'"

Now, I'm watching my nine-year-old, who had just become a Christian the day before. And I know what he's thinking: Sin is all the bad things I do, and when I asked Jesus to live in my heart, He took away my sin. But I know that I still do bad things; for instance, I punched my little brother this morning in the car on the way to Vacation Bible School. So, either it didn't work, and Jesus doesn't live in my heart; or God can't love me, because I still do bad things.

See what I mean? As a result, we try to cover up the "bad things" that still lurk inside us so that God—and His people—will still love us. And we never, ever admit them to anyone. And to deal with our shame we begin doing a lot of "good things" to make up for the bad things. You get a kid thinking like that at age nine, and by the time he's forty-five he's exhausted from trying to "do good." Because you can never be good enough. Sue Bender experiences it this way: "For as long as I can remember I have been listening to a harsh, critical voice inside me, but I've lived with it so long that I never really noticed the influence it was having on my life. I not only listened, I believed what this *harsh judge* was saying.

"The voice passes judgment on *everything* I do.

"'You're not measuring up!' the judge shouts.

"I'm never sure what I am supposed to measure up to, only that I never will.

"Nothing I do will ever be enough."⁵

My youngest son Ben understands this quite well. Ben is a free spirit. He is boisterous and joyous and lives life with gusto. Consequently he had a little trouble getting the hang of school. On Ben's first day in kindergarten, when the teacher said, "It's time to go to your centers," Ben replied, "I don't feel like doing that right now."

By second grade he had become very discouraged. Our school uses a color-coded system of cards for behavior management. Everybody begins the day with a blue card. If you have some trouble in class, you pull a green card. And so on. Orange is the worst color you can get. Orange means you've had a very bad day.

After four orange days in a row, I sighed, "Ben, what is wrong?"

"I don't know!" he moaned. "I want to be blue, but something in my head tells me to be orange!"

"Ben," I said, "that's in the Bible!" We got out his Bible and read Romans 7:15 and 18. "I do not understand what I do. For what I want to do I do not do, but what I hate I do. For I have the desire to do what is good, but I cannot carry it out." We highlighted the whole passage in orange.

"Woe is me!" cried Isaiah. He saw the greatness of God, and he recognized his inability to reproduce it.

"In repentance and rest is your salvation," God says to His people. "In quietness and trust is your strength" (Isa. 30:15). In that passage Isaiah said, "The LORD longs to be gracious to you; he rises to show you compassion" (Isa. 30:18). What is He waiting for? He is waiting for us to remember Who He is, to trust Him. He is waiting for us to ask for His forgiveness. He is waiting for us to acknowledge that He is God. Isaiah, who saw the LORD high and lifted up, proclaimed, "For this is what the high and lofty One says—he who lives forever, whose name is holy: 'I live in a high and holy place, but also with him who is contrite and lowly in spirit'" (Isa. 57:15).

Isaiah was sent out, but not until he had the right perspective.

We must worship before we serve, because worship produces in us two crops that are pleasing and beautiful to God: humility and kindness. Humility shows up in our response to God; kindness is evidenced in our response to others. Humility is knowing we are not up to the journey; kindness is realizing that others are not, either.

The opposite of worship is pride. Pride leads us to serve God for many wrong reasons. Here are three that I know from personal experience.

Wrong Reason #1: Because I have gifts.

Every fall, as the time approaches to volunteer for teaching or leadership positions in my church, I wrestle with this one. I may be exhausted physically and spiritually (so much so that I am hardly more than a "warm body" filling a leadership slot), but I have to keep teaching this class, I think, because I have the gift of teaching.

In part this stems from an inaccurate understanding of spiritual gifts. Somewhere along the line you may have taken a spiritual gifts inventory and identified your gift. Those inventories are useful, especially for discovering our place in the body of Christ. However, they have the danger of pigeonholing believers. Maria has the gift of serving, so she ends up in the kitchen at every church event. Helen has the gift of leadership; she has chaired the same committee for eight years. Both women may be weary of their roles, but they will most likely continue to serve in them because they are so gifted, as everyone continually reminds them.

Spiritual gifts were never intended to be a ball and chain—or a trophy. God gifts believers with supernatural abilities to equip them for the humbling opportunity of co-laboring with Him. He does not empower us in order to obligate us to Himself, nor does He intend our gifts to provide us some ranking or place in the body. In fact, Paul strongly warns of the danger of taking pride in spiritual gifts (1 Cor. 12–13).

Furthermore, God is always doing a new thing and calling us to join Him, which requires new gifts, challenges, and risks. If God requires something new of you, He is entirely able to empower you with a supernatural gift for that job, in that place, at that moment—and later to gift you to do something else. By definition a spiritual gift is a God-given ability to do His work His way. It is not a "use-it-or-lose-it" arrangement; we are stewards of what has been entrusted to us. God knows what you need when you need it, and He will provide it. Whether you are a gifted teacher, servant, leader, administrator, pastor, or counselor is not up to you; it is up to Him.

Wrong Reason #2: **Because I want to be useful.**

When I was a student at Baylor University, a speaker in the morning chapel service made this statement: "My greatest fear is that I will not be useful to God." His words made such an impression on me, I wrote them in the front of my Bible. Years later I read them and cringed. As earnest and sincere as I was, I recognize the ambition in those words. The emphasis was not on God, it was on my usefulness.

"If God wants it to, my life will be useful through my word and witness," wrote an obscure French monk named Dominique Voillaume. "If he wants it to, my life will bear fruit through my prayers and sacrifices. But the usefulness of my life is his concern, not mine. It would be indecent of me to worry about that."[6]

If God is indeed God (and I'm not), then He decides *whether* to use me and *how* to use me. "Who are you, O man, to talk back to God?" Paul reasoned. "Shall what is formed say to him who formed it, 'Why did you make me like this?' " (Rom. 9:20). I may want to be a cup; a cup is *so* useful. But God may intend for me to be a saucer—which also has its uses. Furthermore, if God wants to set me on a shelf and leave me there, that's His prerogative.

Our ambition to be used by God leads us into all kinds of dangerous traps, such as separating out what is and isn't useful to the kingdom. We end up categorizing the activities of life as spiritual or secular. But it is not the job that determines its worth and impact, rather it is the heart of the person approaching and executing the task. No work in itself is spiritual or secular. "God's order is not to abolish the mundane and routine from the life of the Christian, but to transform it," says Jean Fleming.[7]

Pride of usefulness also causes us to judge others. "Lord, what about him?" Peter asked Jesus, referring to John. Wisely (and kindly, I think) Jesus answered, "What is that to you? You must follow me" (John 21:21–22). Edith Schaeffer writes, "God's way of doing things is the measuring stick given to us to measure ourselves by. We are not to use it to judge each other, but to stand directly alone before God and to check up, time after time, on whether or not we are sincerely and practically serving and with the right motives."[8]

Martha of Bethany fell into this trap when Jesus came to visit her home. (See Luke 10.) I don't doubt that Martha was devoted to Jesus, but I venture to guess that she took a fair amount of pride in playing "hostess-with-the-mostest," judging by her reaction when her sister Mary chose to sit in the living room with Jesus. Martha felt that Mary was being useless. Her words echo Peter's: "What about her?" Right after that, Martha uttered the words that reveal she had grown weary in doing good: "I'm the only one doing all the work."

Wrong Reason #3: Because there are needs.

The subject of usefulness and serving would come up again later in Mary and Martha's home, when Mary poured out her expensive bottle of perfume on Jesus' feet. (See John 12:1–8; Mark 14:3–9.) An extravagant gesture. Some said foolish. "It could've been used to feed the poor," one apostle commented piously. Many of us would agree. Jesus' reply ranks among some of His strangest sayings: "The poor you will always have with you, and you can help them any time you want. But you will not always have me."

Was this a momentary lapse of divine character? Was Jesus being selfish and indulgent, callous to the plight of the poor? No. Jesus was penetratingly aware of the needs of the world, and He knew that the truly impoverished are not those who are poor in possessions, but those who are poor in spirit. Looking around that gathering, Jesus saw through the stately robes of the Pharisees and religious leaders to hearts that were starved—hearts so barren and dry they did not even recognize their own God as they sat at the table with Him. But Mary did. Jesus made a breathtaking statement about this woman: "She has done a beautiful thing to me."

What Mary did pleased God. It was beautiful to Him. That, in itself, should be our first and highest ambition.

There will always be needs in our world. Our natural impulse is to run toward the needs. Don't. The God is who is able to do "immeasurably more than all we ask or imagine" (Eph. 3:20) does not need you and me to run ourselves so ragged helping the needy that we become spiritually impoverished ourselves. He will meet every need in Christ Jesus (Phil. 4:19). We are not the Living Water; He is.

Run to the Source. Pour yourself out at His feet—extravagantly, joyfully, tearfully, humbly, lovingly. Pour out everything you treasure—your trophies, your pride, your gifts, talents, ambitions, ministry. Hold nothing back. Spend yourself completely on Him. Don't worry about looking foolish, for Jesus has said, "This is beautiful to me." Don't worry about running dry, for Jesus said, "Whoever drinks the water I give him will never thirst. Indeed, the water I give him will become in him a spring of water welling up to eternal life" (John 4:14). As my friend Edna Ellison says, "Drink until you become the spring." Soak Him up. Drink in His presence until you overflow. He is wonderful! Have you forgotten that? Fix your eyes on Him until He gives you a new way of seeing.

"Now we see but a poor reflection as in a mirror," Paul wrote, "then we shall see face to face" (1 Cor. 13:12). On that day when we stand face-to-face with Jesus, we will indeed have a new way of seeing. And I don't find any job descriptions listed for heaven except one: we will all worship Him. And no one will be weary.

Life is our rehearsal. Practice for heaven.

CHAPTER 4

Growing Weary in Obedience

Oh, the joys of those who do not follow evil men's advice, who do not hang around with sinners. . . . But they delight in doing everything God wants them to, and day and night are always meditating on his laws and thinking about ways to follow him more closely.

They are like trees along a river bank bearing luscious fruit.

—Psalm 1:1–3 TLB

Only he who believes is obedient, and only he who is obedient believes.

—Brennan Manning[1]

I had hoped to put off this chapter until later in this book. I don't want to scare off any readers with what my friends call "The *O* word": obedience. But take a deep breath and plunge in. We must talk about obedience now, because obedience and worship are inexorably linked. What we worship is what, or whom, we obey. G. Campbell Morgan writes: "Every man is bound somewhere, somehow, to a throne, to a government, to an authority, to something that is supreme, to something to which he offers sacrifice, and burns incense, and bends the knee."[2]

That phrase "bends the knee" has new significance for me since corresponding with my friend Sherri, who lives in a country where she cannot safely write the word *pray* in her email. When Sherri wants me to pray about something, she writes, "Please bend the knee." Her prayer warriors are "knee-benders." Sherri and Ben recently adopted twins from a third-world country. It was a long and heart-rending process. At one point the caretaker in the small village where the twins had been born was not willing to give up the baby girl. "The enemy is strong there," Sherri wrote. "She bends the knee to another."

The ancient custom of bowing—bending the knee—means the same thing in all cultures. It indicates place; we bow to the one who is greater than we. We bow to that which is our master. "No one can serve two masters," Jesus said (Matt. 6:24). Joshua put it this way as he spoke to the Israelites who were about to enter the promised land: "Choose for yourselves this day whom you will serve, whether the gods your forefathers served beyond the River, or the gods of the Amorites, in whose land you are living. But as for me and my household, we will serve the LORD" (Josh. 24:15). Like the Israelites, we must choose between the gods of our culture and the one true God who has made it very clear that He will not tolerate idolatry. "You shall have no other gods before me" (Ex. 20:3). Or even alongside Him. "I will not give my glory to another" (Isa. 42:8).

Somebody once said, "Show me your calendar and your checkbook, and I'll tell you what's important to you." This may cut to the quick, but it makes a good point: Everybody worships. The question is what, or whom, do we worship? What is really valuable to us? This will determine our priorities, our choices, and our actions. We spend our energies on what we worship. We sacrifice for it. We adjust our lives to accommodate that which is most important. We are born worshipers. In fact, we were created for that purpose. It is in our nature to commit our hearts to something that makes life worth living and to spend ourselves toward that end—to dream about it, work toward it, train for it, revel in it. We must be very careful where we give our hearts, because true worship requires more than emotion or intention. True devotion to our hearts' desire demands disciplined commitment. It requires obedience. We were made to live this way.

From the very beginning, our Creator is also a covenant-maker. His covenant with humanity is very simple: you obey Me, and I will be with you. But from the very beginning, man has been a covenant-breaker. All Adam and Eve had to do was stay away from two trees. God's covenant with Abraham was, "Obey me, and I will make you the father of many nations." But Sarah had her own plan, and it had disastrous consequences (Gen. 15–18; 21). Henry Blackaby writes, "Your obedience will cost you and others around you."[3] So will your disobedience. Because Sarah ran ahead of God, the children of Ishmael (the Arab nation) and the children of Isaac (the Jewish nation) are still at war. Adam and Eve's disobedience eventually cost God the life of His own Son.

> If you follow my decrees and are careful to obey my commands, I will send you rain in its season, and the ground will yield its crops and the trees of the field their fruit. Your threshing will continue until grape harvest and the grape harvest will continue until planting, and you will eat all the food you want and live in safety in your land.
>
> I will grant peace in the land, and you will lie down and no one will make you afraid. I will remove savage beasts from the land, and the sword will not pass through your country. You will pursue your enemies, and they will fall by the sword before you. Five of you will chase a hundred, and a hundred of you will chase ten thousand, and your enemies will fall by the sword before you.

> I will look on you with favor and make you fruit-
> ful and increase your numbers, and I will keep my
> covenant with you. You will still be eating last year's
> harvest when you will have to move it out to make
> room for the new. I will put my dwelling place
> among you, and I will not abhor you (Lev. 26:3–11).

The heart of every promise God has made is "I will be with you." Jesus' very name fulfilled this covenant: *Emmanuel* means "God with us." "If anyone loves me," Jesus said, "he will obey my teaching. My Father will love him, and we will come to him and make our home with him" (John 14:23). "Let not your heart be troubled," He assured His disciples, "I will not leave you as orphans; I will come to you" (John 14:1, 18 NASB). The last words He spoke to them on earth were, "I am with you always" (Matt. 28:20). God's hymn at the close of time is: "Now the dwelling of God is with men, and he will live with them. They will be his people, and God himself will be with them and be their God" (Rev. 21:3).

Obey me, and I will be with you. Implied in this covenant is God's promise "and if I am with you, that will be enough." If we have God, we have everything we need. This is our security, our peace, our rest. When we go running after other gods or choose our own way, we forfeit this security. The truth is that no other god will come through for us. There is no other god like ours. The fact that we do not obey Him indicates that we do not know Him.

When we obey Him, we come to know Him better. Every time we walk through something with Him, we see a new facet of Him through that experience. I am nailed by my pastor's recent comments on Psalm 23:4 ("Even though I walk through the valley of the shadow of death"). Mike admits he is more inclined to say, "Even though I blow through the valley of the shadow of death." Sometimes our obedience to God is difficult, even frightening, and we would like to get it over quickly. But if we "blow through" the valley, we miss knowing the comfort of the Shepherd who is with us. The psalmist David chose two interesting and revealing images for this comfort: the rod and the staff. The familiar shepherd's staff with its crook was used to rescue a sheep who had wandered or fallen into danger. The rod (or club) was used to defend against other animals and to correct stubborn sheep. Of both instruments of discipline, David said, "They comfort me." Ironically, obedience is ultimately comforting, because through it we come to know the Shepherd who disciplines and defends us. When I am unwilling or slow to obey, I need to back up and get to know God.

In *Experiencing God* by Henry Blackaby,[3] I learned that there are three things we must know about God if we are to trust Him enough to obey Him. First, God is all-wise; nothing ever happens outside His comprehension. Just because I don't know what's coming next, I shouldn't assume God doesn't know. I may not understand what is happening, but God does.

Nothing ever takes God by surprise. Think about that. He is never thrown for a loop. In the seventies, in the early days of the television show *Saturday Night Live,* there was a funny sketch about a family called "The Fraid Family." The Fraids were afraid of everything. If the phone or the doorbell rang, their hair would stand on end, they would throw up their hands and say, "Oh no! It might be a robber," or some other worrisome possibility.

Listen to me: God never throws His hands up and shouts, "Oh no!" When something you didn't expect occurs, it does not put a kink in His plan. "For my thoughts are not your thoughts," God reminds us, "neither are your ways my ways" (Isa. 55:8).

If we are to trust God enough to obey Him, the second thing we must know is that God is all-powerful; He is able to handle any circumstance. This is how the boy David faced the giant Goliath. "You come against me with sword and spear and javelin, but I come against you in the name of the LORD Almighty"

(1 Sam. 17:45). "The LORD is my light and my salvation," wrote David, "whom shall I fear?" (Psalm 27:1). The Apostle Paul understood this when he wrote, "We are more than conquerors through him who loved us. . . . If God is for us," Paul reasoned, "who can be against us?" (Rom. 8:31–37). With this same conviction, he wrote to the church in Ephesus: "I keep asking that the God of our Lord Jesus Christ, the glorious Father, may give you the Spirit of wisdom and revelation, *so that you may know him better.* I pray also that the eyes of your heart may be enlightened in order that you may know the hope to which he has called you, the riches of his glorious inheritance in the saints, and his incomparably great power for us who believe" (Eph. 1:17–19, italics mine).

Paul went on to say that this great power available to us is the same power that God exerted when He raised Christ from the dead and seated Him on the throne in heaven! Do you know that? If not, I pray that the eyes of your heart will be opened to see the greatness of your God. This is your inheritance, Isaiah promised: "No weapon forged against you will prevail" (Isa. 54:17).

If we are to trust God enough to obey Him, the third thing we must know is that God is all-loving; He only works for good. "Every good and perfect gift is from above, coming down from the Father of the heavenly lights, who does not change like shifting shadows" (James 1:17). God does not sometimes send good and sometimes send bad. He does not have a bad day and decide to take it out on us. God is love, 1 John 4:16 tells us. To act any other way toward us would be to deny His own essence. As I said in the introduction to this book, God is the definition of good.

Now, there are times when what is going on doesn't feel good. When God waits to act (because He is all-wise and knows something I don't), I get impatient and question whether what is happening to me matters to Him. When God allows pain and suffering to continue in the world (when I know He is all-powerful and could stop it if He chose), I wonder if He is either just out of touch with His creation or else has grown hard-hearted. When I doubt God, I begin to look around for other more congenial masters who I think might come through for me. Oh, I don't say, "I'm going to find myself another god." But very subtly I begin to place my confidence elsewhere: in my career, in my achievements, in the approval of others. A relationship. A bank account. A Mastercard. (They don't call it Mastercard for nothing; once you begin to rely on it, it masters you!) Nice church-going people like you and me don't think of ourselves as idolaters, but God makes it clear that to covenant with anyone or anything else—to agree to their terms—is idolatry.

Why is God such a stickler for our undivided loyalty and obedience?

First, because when we rely solely on Him and He provides for us, He gets the glory. When we do things His way, the results are unexplainable, except that He must be who He says He is. When we obey God, others see the result, and they have to reckon with Him, which is what He wants. When we belong to God and obey Him, His reputation is at stake before others. He will defend His good name. He will prove Himself. When we obey God, we witness to others.

Almost ten years ago Dennis and I made the decision to end a full-time public ministry that required us to live on the road. We did not know what we would do next, but we clearly felt God say it was time to stop, so we trusted that He would provide what we needed next. For nearly a year, as we continued to meet the commitments on the road that were already in place, we waited for God to reveal the next thing. One month before our last known source of income, I was beginning to get nervous and more than a little impatient. I stomped around the house, asking God what He was up to. I pounded my fist and asked Him why He was leaving us hanging out on this limb.

"Ooh, Karla's mad," teased a friend. "God's scared."

No, He wasn't. He was quite calm because, unlike me, He knew what was coming next. And He knew something else that I didn't—there were more important issues at stake than whether the Worleys had income or not.

It was during this time that my brother and his wife moved to live near us. My sister-in-law, not a Christian at the time, was new to the church world. She was watching and trying to make sense of us and our God. Kim told me later that one of the reasons she began to take God seriously was the way we had made this career decision. She had never seen anyone evaluate life based on obedience to God rather than money or career goals. Although she did see how we shook in our boots, she also saw God meet every need and more. It was one of her first steps toward accepting Him as her own Savior and Lord.

God knew His reputation was at stake, and He used our obedience, shaky as it was, to display His faithfulness. As Psalm 23:3 says, "He restores my soul. He guides me in paths of righteousness *for his name's sake*" (italics mine).

One of the central aspects of God's character is His righteousness—a big church word we hear and repeat, but can't clearly define. Romans 3:22 tells us this righteousness from God comes through faith in Jesus Christ to all who believe. We believers are often referred to as "the righteous."

God's righteousness is His ability to keep His covenant. It is His faithfulness to defend His name and to defend those who bear His name. God's covenant with us is "Obey me, and I will be with you." His righteousness guarantees that He will keep that promise. He will always be with us, provide for us, empower us, defend us, discipline us, teach us, guide us, love us. God never fails to keep His end of the covenant. Not ever. That is His righteousness.

Unfortunately, "righteousness" has been muddied by our tendency toward self-righteousness. We inaccurately translate "righteousness" as "right-ness"—those who "do right" are righteous.

Self-righteousness is what we exhibit when we become impressed with our own ability to "do right." Few things weary us more than self-righteousness—the attempt to make ourselves obey. In an effort to "get right" or "be right" with God, we invent extra rules and regulations. We steel ourselves to be obedient; we grit our teeth to follow God. However, God's Word informs us that "there is no one righteous, not even one" (Rom. 3:10).

Our part of the covenant is to do one thing: obey Him. And there is not one human being who has ever lived or ever will live who has the ability to keep his or her end of this bargain. Not one. All have sinned—willfully disobeyed (Rom. 3:23) It is only when Jesus Christ lives in us that the Holy Spirit produces in us the fruit called righteousness—the ability to obey. Our obedience is proof that Christ lives in us, that we belong to God.

> We know that we have come to know him if we obey his commands. The man who says, "I know him," but does not do what he commands is a liar, and the truth is not in him. But if anyone obeys his word, God's love is truly made complete in him. This is how we know we are in him: Whoever claims to live in him must walk as Jesus did (1 John 2:3–6).

"'Woe to the obstinate children,' declares the LORD, 'to those who carry out plans that are not mine.' These are rebellious people, deceitful children, children unwilling to listen to the LORD's instruction" (Isa. 30:1, 9). This phrase "deceitful children" can be translated "false sons"—in other words, people who pretend to be God's children but whose behavior proves otherwise. The theologian Soren Kierkegaard once described two kinds of Christians: those who imitate Jesus Christ and those who are content to speak about Him.[4] Jesus made it clear that lip service is not enough. "Not everyone who says to me, 'Lord, Lord,' will enter the kingdom of heaven, but only he who does the will of my Father" (Matt. 7:21).

My youngest sons have just spent a week with their Grammer Worley in Texas, where they have met cousins, aunts, and uncles who had never seen them before. Apparently, their relatives had no trouble recognizing them. "I'd know him anywhere," said one aunt. "He acts just like his daddy."

When we live in a covenant relationship with our God, people recognize Him in the way we act and the way He responds. And here's a scary thought: God also demonstrates His righteousness by separating Himself from us when our disobedience dishonors His name. Does God forgive disobedience? Certainly. But He does not indulge it. Every promise God makes has a condition, and the condition for receiving God's presence, protection, and provision is "if you obey."

> This is what the LORD says—your Redeemer, the Holy One of Israel: "I am the LORD your God, who teaches you what is best for you, who directs you in the way you should go. If only you had paid attention to my commands, your peace would have been like a river, your righteousness like the waves of the sea. Your descendants would have been like the sand, your children like its numberless grains; their name would never be cut off nor destroyed from before me" (Isa. 48:17–19).

God also requires obedience in order to protect us. Because God made us, He knows that our nature, like His, is to be in covenant relationship. There is a God-given need in us to belong, and we will covenant with any master who makes us a good offer. But God is the only Master who loves His servants and is concerned with their welfare. "The law of the Lord is perfect, reviving the soul," proclaims Psalm 19:7. But "idols speak deceit, diviners see visions that lie; they tell dreams that are false, they give comfort in vain. Therefore the people wander like sheep oppressed for lack of a shepherd" (Zech. 10:2).

The result of obedience to God is peace. "'There is no peace,' says the LORD, 'for the wicked'" (Isa. 48:22). Who exactly are the wicked? The word used here means "willfully disobedient." That includes us. When we disobey God, even in little things, we have no peace, no rest—we are literally restless.

> Then the LORD will scatter you among all nations, from one end of the earth to the other. There you will worship other gods—gods of wood and stone, which neither you nor your fathers have known. Among those nations you will find no repose, no resting place for the sole of your foot. There the LORD will give you an anxious mind, eyes weary with longing, and a despairing heart. You will live in constant suspense, filled with dread both night and day, never sure of your life (Deut. 28:64–66).

There have been times in my life when I felt "the peace that transcends all understanding," that Paul described in Philippians 4:7—not because everything was going smoothly, or all my questions were answered, but because I knew I was walking hand-in-hand with God. Although the circumstances of my life were challenging, I was not struggling with who was in charge. For once, I was cooperating with God, confident that He was working out His will. If you have ever walked through a period of time like that, you know that there is an unexplainable peace that accompanies it. Obeying God produces in us the spiritual fruit of peace, a pleasing crop. Lack of peace is God's way of telling us that we are out of covenant with Him. "Blessed is he whose transgressions are forgiven, whose sins are covered," David sang. "Blessed is the man whose sin the LORD does not count against him and in whose spirit is no deceit" (Psalm 32:1–2).

When David fell in love with Bathsheba, he had her husband Uriah sent to the battlefront so that Uriah would be killed and David would have Bathsheba for himself. This "man after God's own heart" chose what he wanted over what God commanded. I've been there. Once I even made a list of pros and cons when I was struggling to obey God in a money matter. I wanted to buy something very badly, but we had committed to a strict budget in order to eliminate debt. On one side of sheet, I listed "Reasons I Should Do What God Says," and on the other side of the sheet I listed "Reasons I Should Do What I Want." I had at least ten reasons to obey God, not the least of which was "because He said so." I had only one reason to disobey: "because I want it." The thing is, that one reason on my side of the page weighed in as heavily as the long list on God's side of the page.

What happens when we willfully disobey God? We have to shut out His voice and put up a wall of pretense. We have to dull our senses and jam our schedules with enough activity and noise that He can't get through to us. We have to create our own version of reality, with all the accompanying lies and false fronts this demands. You can wear yourself out trying to ignore God.

"When I kept silent," David continued in Psalm 32, "my bones wasted away through my groaning all day long. For day and night your hand was heavy upon me; my strength was sapped as in the heat of summer. Then I acknowledged my sin to you and did not cover up my iniquity. I said, 'I will confess my transgressions to the LORD'—and you forgave the guilt of my sin" (vv. 3-5).

Have you ever felt God's hand heavy upon you, felt something gnawing at the edge of your day, and as you tossed and turned with no sleep in the night? "I cried out to God for help; I cried out to

God to hear me," wailed the psalmist. "When I was in distress, I sought the Lord; at night I stretched out untiring hands and my soul refused to be comforted. I remembered you, O God, and I groaned; I mused, and my spirit grew faint. You kept my eyes from closing; I was too troubled to speak" (Psalm 77:1–4).

What a pitiful image—hands reaching, reaching for comfort, but receiving none. The child in the night, crying out for the comfort of her parent's presence. The cry of Christ on the cross: "Why have you forsaken me?" For the first and only time, Jesus was separated from His Father at that moment when "God made him who had no sin to be sin for us, so that in him we might become the righteousness of God" (2 Cor. 5:21). The One who came to fulfill God's covenant, the One who was "God with us," felt God turn His back, and it was horrible. He stretched out His hands, and there was no comfort. There was no parent. There was no presence. There was no peace.

Sometimes this voice that keeps you awake in the night is the voice of the accuser, who does his best to discourage us. One of his most effective tools is to dredge up our old sins, to replay the stupid blunders, the selfish choices, the hurtful actions of our past. Since Satan cannot take away our salvation, he'll try to make us doubt our standing. Be very careful that you recognize whose voice is speaking. The voice of God reminds us of our sin only in order to bring us back to Him. That's why Jesus said, "Blessed are those who mourn, for they will be comforted" (Matt. 5:4).

The word *blessed* is *marakoi*, and it does not read "happy." It is translated "God is fully present with." And the word *mourn* means to grieve over sin. Lamentations expresses this kind of mourning.

> My sins have been bound into a yoke; by his hands they were woven together. They have come upon my neck and the Lord has sapped my strength. He has handed me over to those I cannot withstand.

Zion stretches out her hands, but there is no one to comfort her. The LORD has decreed for Jacob that his neighbors become his foes; Jerusalem has become an unclean thing among them. The LORD is righteous, yet I rebelled against his command (Lam. 1:14, 17–18).

Lamentations, which we don't often read, is a book of wailings that were read annually by the Jews as a reminder of the fall of Jerusalem and the destruction of the temple—probably the most shameful time in the history of the Jewish nation. These laments were a reminder of the terrible consequences of sin and the righteousness of God, who keeps His covenant. From this book come the words we sing so often: "Because of the LORD's great love we are not consumed, for his compassions never fail. They are new every morning; great is your faithfulness" (Lam. 3:22–23).

"The path to peace is paved with knee-prints," wrote Beth Moore.[5] God is fully present to those who grieve over their sin, repent, and bend the knee to Him again. The question is, how badly do you want what you want? Enough to shut God out, to erect a wall of rationalization? The heart is deceitful; repentance does not come naturally. David knew this firsthand, and he came to pray in a new way: "Search me, O God, and know my heart; test me and know my anxious thoughts. See if there is any offensive way in me, and lead me in the way everlasting. Forgive my hidden faults. Keep your servant also from willful sins; may they not rule over me" (Psalms 139:23–24; 19:12–13).

It takes this kind of intentional surrender to live in covenant with God. Obedience is God's line in the dust. God takes sin very seriously, and so should we.

"Be very careful, then, how you live—not as unwise, but as wise," Paul advised. "Do not be foolish, but understand what the Lord's will is" (Eph. 5:15–17). While none of us would choose to live foolishly, we often do so because we fail to purposefully consider God in our daily choices. At the end of his life David advised his son Solomon, who would succeed him as king and build the temple: "And you, my son Solomon, acknowledge the God of your father, and serve him with wholehearted devotion and with a willing mind, for the LORD searches every heart and understands every motive behind the thoughts. If you seek him, he will be found by you; but if you forsake him, he will reject you forever" (1 Chron. 28:9).

In his first act as king, Solomon assembled all the leaders of the kingdom at the Tent of Meeting and bowed down to worship God at the altar there.

That night God appeared to Solomon and said to him, "Ask for whatever you want me to give you."

> Solomon answered God, "You have shown great kindness to David my father and have made me king in his place. Now, LORD God, let your promise to my father David be confirmed, for you have made me king over a people who are as numerous as the dust of the earth. Give me wisdom and knowledge, that I may lead this people, for who is able to govern this great people of yours?"
>
> God said to Solomon, "Since this is your heart's desire and you have not asked for wealth, riches or honor, nor for the death of your enemies, and since you have not asked for a long life but for wisdom and knowledge to govern my people over whom I have made you king, therefore wisdom and knowledge will be given you. And I will also give you wealth, riches and honor, such as no king who was before you ever had and none after you will have" (2 Chron. 1:7–12).

What Solomon asked for, literally, was a "hearing heart." Up close and personal, he had seen the enormous task of ruling. He had witnessed his brothers' attempt to overthrow their own father, army after army coming after the kingdom. He had watched as his father David, a man devoted to God, was led astray by his own heart, and Solomon had lived among the devastating results of David's disobedience. "Who is able to govern these people?" he admitted. So Solomon asked for wisdom—the ability to hear God. A hearing heart.

In the Bible, "hearing" implies the intent to obey. Isaiah described this relationship: "He wakens me morning by morning, wakens my ear to listen like one being taught. The Sovereign LORD has opened my ears, and I have not been rebellious; I have not drawn back" (Isa. 50:4–5). When the Apostle Paul wrote to the Ephesians, "Be careful how you live," he was saying in effect, "Live as hearing, not as unhearing" (Eph. 5:15, my paraphrase). The word *absurd* comes from the Latin *surdus*, meaning "deaf." *Obedience* comes from the Latin *ob audire*, meaning "to listen to." As Brennan Manning wrote: "Our lives may be filled to overflowing—so many events and commitments that we wonder how we'll get it all done. Yet at the same time, we might feel unfulfilled and wonder if anything is worth living for. Being filled yet unfulfilled, busy yet bored, involved yet lonely, these are the symptoms of the absurd lifestyle that makes us inattentive to spiritual realities."[6]

How do you get a hearing heart? Ask for it. "If any of you lacks wisdom, he should ask God, who gives generously to all without finding fault, and it will be given to him" (James 1:5). The ability to hear and obey comes from God, and as we can see from Solomon's experience, God is delighted to give it.

Can you picture that scene? With troops, generals, strategists and advisers, priests and teachers watching, the great king of Israel, newly coronated, commander-in-chief of all the armies, bent his knee before the greater King. He laid his offerings before the Lord

Almighty, and by this Solomon showed the nation who was really in charge. "The fear of the LORD is the beginning of [a hearing heart]," declares Psalm 111:10. As we have said, the fear of the Lord is knowing who is in charge and who is not. My own sons often yell at each other, "You are not the boss of me!"

Trying to boss one another is exhausting. Trying to boss God is even more exhausting. We do this when we attempt to keep Him in a box—to say, "This far you may come, and no farther. This part of me you may boss, but this part I'm keeping for myself." As I once heard a preacher say, "There is no such sentence as, 'No, Lord.'" Either He is Lord, or He is not. To say no is to say He is not Lord.

We try to boss God when we set conditions upon our service:

> As they were walking along the road, a man said to him, "I will follow you wherever you go." Jesus replied, "Foxes have holes and birds of the air have nests, but the Son of Man has no place to lay his head." He said to another man, "Follow me." But the man replied, "Lord, first let me go and bury my father." Jesus said to him, "Let the dead bury their own dead, but you go and proclaim the kingdom of God." Still another said, "I will follow you, Lord; but first let me go back and say good-bye to my family." Jesus replied, "No one who puts his hand to the plow and looks back is fit for service in the kingdom of God" (Luke 9:57–62).

It's interesting that Jesus did not say, "Believe me," or "Bow down to me," when He called His disciples. He simply invited them, "Follow me." Go with me. Let's walk and talk. Get to know me. Watch what I do. Join me. It is the most demanding thing He could ask. "I'd like to have quiet time," we answer, "but I have these children . . . " "I'd help with this ministry, but my job demands so much . . . . " You cannot continue life as usual or stay where you are, and go with God at the same time. As long as we put off obeying Him, we will never come to know Him. A distinguishing mark of the disciples who came to know Christ intimately was that "at once they left their nets and followed him" (Matt. 4:20).

"You did not choose me," Jesus reminded His disciples. "I chose you, and appointed you to go and bear fruit—fruit that will last" (John 15:16). The servant doesn't choose his task, nor the time and place he will do it. We will never find a moment when it's convenient to obey God. We must arrange our lives to accommodate Him, not the other way around. Take the story of the prophet Jonah, for instance.

Now, I'm a full-fledged member of the "me" generation. What's in it for me? How will this affect me? And the religious version: What is God's will for me? So I understand why, when God said, "Go to Nineveh," Jonah immediately looked to see what was in it for him. All he could see was trouble. Nineveh was a wicked city, capital of Israel's powerful enemy, Assyria. Jonah hopped a ship in the opposite direction. You know the story: a storm came up, the sailors tossed Jonah overboard, he was swallowed up by a giant fish, and after three days in its belly, Jonah repented. (Wouldn't you have done the same?) Jonah went to Nineveh. He delivered God's message, and the people repented and were spared.

Two things strike me about this story: First, God accomplished His will as effectively in Jonah's disobedience as in his obedience (Jonah 1:8–16; 3:1–10). Second, Jonah still missed the point, considering only how it affected him (Jonah 4). God uses clueless people. I know; I am one! But when reputation or comfort is my priority, I miss the joy of being God's vessel. "Those who cling to worthless idols forfeit the grace that could be theirs," Jonah admitted from inside the fish (Jonah 2:8). Those who cling to their own comfort forfeit the joy that could be theirs. "Your attitude should be the same as that of Christ Jesus," Paul wrote. Although

He was equal with God, Jesus did not insist on His own rights. Instead, "he humbled himself and became obedient to death— even death on a cross!" (Phil. 2:5, 8). "The one who sent me is with me," Jesus said. "He has not left me alone, for I always do what pleases him" (John 8:29).

We boss God when we tell Him in our prayers what to do. I laugh when someone sends me a prayer request that says, "Pray that God will . . . . " I have done this myself; one particular instance stands out. I was at a Tuesday evening Bible study group, and as we were closing in prayer, I told the group that I was in for a long night ahead. I had an article due to my publisher the next day that I hadn't even started. "Just pray that God will help me stay up all night and give me the words to say," I instructed my group.

On the way home, I was busy talking to God. "Now, Lord, you've just got to help me. I've got to pull an all-nighter. Just get my kids to bed early and keep me from interruptions, so I can get this done." Then God spoke to me. (Mind you, He did not speak out loud, but I knew who was speaking!)

"I didn't tell you to do that," God said, "so I'm not exactly sure why I should help you get it done."

"But, Lord," I argued, "I told them I would do it!"

"Yes," God replied, "but you didn't ask Me first."

"Well, what am I supposed to do now?" I asked.

"I think you should call them up tomorrow and tell them you overcommitted yourself without checking with Me, and you're awfully ashamed, but you can't keep your commitment."

Ouch, that really hurt. I did it, but not without swallowing a lot of pride.

Philippians 4:6 says, "In everything, by prayer and petition, with thanksgiving, present your requests to God," not your instructions to God. We forget our place when we tell God what to do. Notice how these people in the Gospel accounts presented their requests to Jesus:

🖊 Some men came, bringing to him a paralytic, carried by four of them. Since they could not get him to Jesus because of the crowd, they made an opening in the roof above Jesus and, after digging through it, lowered the mat the paralyzed man was lying on. When Jesus saw their faith, he said to the paralytic, "Son, your sins are forgiven" (Mark 2:3–5).

🖊 On the third day a wedding took place at Cana in Galilee. Jesus' mother was there, and Jesus and his disciples had also been invited to the wedding. When the wine was gone, Jesus' mother said to him, "They have no more wine." "Dear woman, why do you involve me?" Jesus replied. "My time has not yet come." His mother said to the servants, "Do whatever he tells you" (John 2:1–5).

🖊 When Jesus had entered Capernaum, a centurion came to him, asking for help. "Lord," he said, "my servant lies at home paralyzed and in terrible suffering."

Jesus said to him, "I will go and heal him."

The centurion replied, "Lord, I do not deserve to have you come under my roof. But just say the word, and my servant will be healed. For I myself am a man under authority, with soldiers under me. I tell this one, 'Go,' and he goes; and that one, 'Come,' and he comes. I say to my servant, 'Do this,' and he does it."

When Jesus heard this, he was astonished and said to those following him, "I tell you the truth, I have not found anyone in Israel with such great faith" (Matt. 8:5–13).

"There is no more wine." "My servant is suffering." The paralytic's friends had no words; they simply brought their friend into Christ's presence. He knew exactly what to do in response. It's no wonder we find prayer so difficult, even wearisome, when we are trying to shoulder the responsibility of telling God what to do!

The weekend before Thanksgiving 1999, my husband, Dennis, was severely injured in a head-on collision, requiring surgery and months of rehabilitation. Dennis is the minister of worship at our church, and many people in our congregation prayed for him during this time. Perhaps the most touching prayers came from our friends Mike and Melanie Lawrence's children, Jacob and Joshua. The boys missed "Mr. Dennis" in the worship services.

"We should pray for him," they told their mother.

Melanie bowed her head with her small sons, and this is what Jacob prayed: "God, Dennis. Amen."

Jacob Lawrence has profoundly changed my prayer life, as I have learned to stop giving God a list of instructions, but simply come to Him to lift someone up or state the situation. I have shared this story at conferences and experienced some of the deepest moments of prayer as we stood around the room quietly and heard the names and needs held up to our Father: "God, Sherri. God, Dan. God, Anita. God, Stephen. Amen." Bringing these to God's attention, we trusted that He knew what to do.

Do you trust Him? This is the heart of obedience. Do you truly believe that He is able to do a better job with your life—and the lives of your loved ones—than you can? The one who arm-wrestles God will wear herself out, but the one who surrenders control will find Him faithful.

In Psalm 32, David's beautiful song about his own struggle to obey, the last refrain is sung by God Himself. It is a chorus full of hope—for David and for all of us:

> I will instruct you and teach you in the way you should go; I will counsel you and watch over you.
>
> Do not be like the horse or the mule, which have no understanding but must be controlled by bit and bridle or they will not come to you.
>
> Many are the woes of the [willfully disobedient], but the LORD's unfailing love surrounds the man who trusts in him (Psalm 32:8–10).

CHAPTER 5

Growing Weary Without Truth

The Sovereign LORD has given me an instructed tongue, to know the word that sustains the weary.
—Isaiah 50:4

This is God's Word for God's people; hear it, believe it, and live it.

—Michael Glenn

*O*ne shining spring day, Seth pointed to the sky. "Yook, Mommy," he said, "the sun."

"Yes, the sun."

"God is in the sun," Seth stated matter-of-factly.

Uh...

"No, honey," I corrected. "God made the sun."

"My Sunny school teacher said, 'God is IN the sun,'" he insisted.

She had said that very thing. It sounded good but wasn't accurate. If you have spent any time in Sunday school or other study groups, you have probably absorbed similar misstatements.

Most likely they were unintentional or misinformed.

Nevertheless, they were wrong, and wrong thinking leads to wrong living. And wrong living leads to weariness.

"Have nothing to do with godless myths and old wives' tales; rather, train yourself to be godly," Paul wrote to Timothy (1 Tim. 4:7). In Paul's day, Jesus' teachings were passed along orally.

Naturally, some folk religion had crept in. We have our own mix of folk religion and truth, such as, "God helps those who help themselves," or "He will never give us anything we cannot bear." It's important that we know God's Word accurately and recognize God's ways, carefully weighing every teaching we receive against the unchanging Word of God.

This is not the prevailing standard of our culture. The last thing we want to hear is that there is an absolute, that we must abide by it. Our culture will tell us that ethics are situational. If a boundary makes us uncomfortable or unhappy, we just move the line. You do your thing; I'll do mine. This is why Christianity is so hard for many. If you accept God's Word as the authoritative source of truth, if you consider His precepts the definitive ethical and moral standard, you are in direct opposition to the culture in which you live. You are swimming upstream. And this is exactly what Jesus prayed for you.

> I gave them your word;
> The godless world hated them because of it,
> Because they didn't join the world's ways,
> Just as I didn't join the world's ways.
> I'm not asking that you take them out of the world
> But that you guard them from the Evil One.
> They are no more defined by the world
> Than I am defined by the world.
> Make them holy—consecrated—with the truth;
> Your word is consecrating truth
> (John 17:14–17 *The Message*).

In the garden of Gethsemane, during His last private hours before His arrest, trial, and crucifixion, Jesus made some personal requests, not just for those with Him at the time, but also for us—"those who will believe in me through their message" (John

17:20). He did not beg God to make it easy for us, to help us fit in or be popular. In fact, He asked just the opposite: Set them apart with the truth. That's what *consecrate* means. Jesus prayed that God's truth would set us apart from the rest of the world—that it would define us as it had defined Him. God's Word makes us different.

Of course, this is the proverbial good news and bad news. First the bad news: Being different is uncomfortable for us and those around us.

When my darling friend Leigh Marie was a teenager, she showed up one afternoon on my doorstep awash in tears. I listened to her pour her heart out about best friends, boy friends, school—everything was difficult at the moment. She just didn't fit in.

"Leigh," I began, taking her beautiful face in my hands, "you are so special. You will never be like everyone else."

"Yeah?" she snuffled. "Well, being special stinks."

You know that's true if you have ever been the one who is different. Different hair. Different nose. Different name. Different background. A different set of values.

> This is the verdict: Light has come into the world, but men loved darkness instead of light because their deeds were evil. Everyone who does evil hates the light, and will not come into the light for fear that his deeds will be exposed. But whoever lives by the truth comes into the light, so that it may be seen plainly that what he has done has been done through God (John 3:19–21).

These verses always remind me of Stephen Hicks, a very funny guy who was traveling with the Bill Gaither Trio at the same time I was, in the 1980s. Stephen was an early riser, so he would wake up long before the rest of us on the bus and entertain himself for several hours. When he could no longer stand it, Stephen would jerk open the curtains to our dark berths, leaving us blinking and squinting into the morning sun, while shouting, "And men hated the light, for their deeds were evil!"

That's exactly the picture John paints of what happens when Jesus Christ shines the light of truth into the dark corners where people keep their secrets. Man does not want to be awakened from his comfortable ignorance, nor does he want his hiding places exposed.

- They say to the seers, "See no more visions!" and to the prophets, "Give us no more visions of what is right! Tell us pleasant things, prophesy illusions. Leave this way, get off this path, and stop confronting us with the Holy One of Israel!" (Isa. 30:10–11).
- For the time will come when men will not put up with sound doctrine. Instead, to suit their own desires, they will gather around them a great number of teachers to say what their itching ears want to hear. They will turn their ears away from the truth and turn aside to myths (2 Tim. 4:3–4).

"The Word of God is living and active," says the writer of Hebrews. "Sharper than any double-edged sword, it penetrates even to dividing soul and spirit, joints and marrow; it judges the thoughts and attitudes of the heart" (Heb. 4:12). The kind of procedure described here is surgery, and if you have ever had surgery—medical or spiritual—you know that it is both frightening and painful.

C. S. Lewis described this surgery in a chilling yet beautiful way in *The Voyage of the Dawn Treader*, the fifth story in his Chronicles of Narnia series. The ship, *Dawn Treader,* landed upon the shores of a strange island, where one of the children on board, Eustace, discovered the lair of a dead dragon, piled with treasure. Eustace filled his pockets with loot until he was so exhausted he fell asleep. With horror he awoke to find that "sleeping on a dragon's hoard with greedy, dragonish thoughts in his heart, he had become a dragon himself." Later in the story he described the process by which he encountered the lion Aslan and became a boy again:

> I was terribly afraid of it. You may think that, being a dragon, I could have knocked any lion out easily enough. But it wasn't that kind of fear. I wasn't afraid of it eating me, I was just afraid of it—if you can understand. Well, it came close up to me and looked straight into my eyes. And I shut my eyes tight. But that wasn't any good because it told me to follow it.
>
> . . . So at last we came to the top of a mountain I'd never seen before and on the top of this mountain there was a garden—trees and fruit and everything. In the middle of it there was a well.
>
> . . . The water was as clear as anything and I thought if I could get in there and bathe it would ease the pain in my leg. But the lion told me I must undress first.

Eustace scratched at his dragon scales until he shed his skin three times, only to find it no good; another suit of scales lay underneath.

> Then the lion said . . . "You will have to let me undress you." I was afraid of his claws, I can tell you, but I was pretty nearly desperate now. So I just lay flat down on my back to let him do it.
>
> The very first tear he made was so deep that I thought it had gone right into my heart. And when he began pulling the skin off, it hurt worse than

anything I've ever felt. The only thing that made me able to bear it was just the pleasure of feeling the stuff peel off . . . .

Well, he peeled the beastly stuff right off—just as I thought I'd done it myself the other three times, only they hadn't hurt—and there it was lying on the grass . . . And there I was as smooth and soft as a peeled switch and smaller than I had been. Then he caught hold of me—I didn't like that much for I was very tender underneath now that I'd no skin on— and threw me into the water. It smarted like anything but only for a moment . . . And then I saw why. I'd turned into a boy again.[1]

"It is a dreadful thing to fall into the hands of the living God," reads Hebrews 10:31. This seems a stark contrast to the God who speaks in Isaiah 49:15–16: "Can a mother forget the baby at her breast and have no compassion on the child she has borne? Though she may forget, I will not forget you! See, I have engraved you on the palms of my hands." In Old Testament times, when a woman was betrothed she would engrave (tattoo) the name of her future husband on the palm of her hand—a painful version of the engagement ring! This would signify that she belonged to him, but also served to bring him to mind during the course of her daily tasks.

Quite a romantic image, to think of ourselves as engraved on the palm of God's hand, constantly on His mind. But remember that the palm of His hand is where the spike was driven on the cross. To belong to Christ means that our name is obliterated and replaced with the scars of His sacrifice.

Every lie, every illusion, every pleasantry we tell ourselves requires a new suit of armor, a new layer of protective skin, the scales of a false reality. Truth tears away our protective layers and exposes our vulnerable, naked realities. This is why people squirm in God's presence. "Surely you desire truth in the inner parts," David wrote (Psalm 51:6), but this is not what we desire. Truth rocks our world.

There is a stunning example of this in John's account of Jesus' trial interrogation by the Roman governor Pontius Pilate (John 18:28–40). As the two men faced each other, Jesus told Pilate, "I have come to bear witness to the truth."

"What is truth?" Pilate fired back. In that moment, I wonder if Pilate looked into Jesus' eyes and heard the unspoken answer: "I AM the Truth." Did he know that Jesus could read him like a book, that Christ could see that Pilate was being used by the High Priest? Did Pilate recognize he was in the presence of a true King and realize how pitifully he compared? Did he sense true authority in this curious prisoner? Did he read the compassion in that bruised and swollen face? Jesus said nothing. He didn't need to. Pilate's answer was looking into His eyes.

🖊 O LORD, you have searched me and you know me. You know when I sit and when I rise; you perceive my thoughts from afar. You discern my going out and my lying down; you are familiar with all my ways. Before a word is on my tongue you know it completely, O LORD. You hem me in—behind and before; you have laid your hand upon me.

Where can I go from your Spirit? Where can I flee from your presence? If I go up to the heavens, you are there; if I make my bed in the depths, you are there. If I rise on the wings of the dawn, if I settle on the far side of the sea, even there your hand will guide me, your right hand will hold me fast.

If I say, "Surely the darkness will hide me and the light become night around me," even the darkness will not be dark to you; the night will shine like the day, for darkness is as light to you (Psalm 139:1–12).

- He changes times and seasons; he sets up kings and deposes them. He gives wisdom to the wise and knowledge to the discerning. He reveals deep and hidden things; he knows what lies in darkness, and light dwells with him (Dan. 2:21–22).
- If you call out for insight and cry aloud for understanding, and if you look for it as for silver and search for it as for hidden treasure, then you will understand the fear of the LORD and find the knowledge of God (Prov. 2:3–5).
- I will give you the treasures of darkness, riches stored in secret places, so that you may know that I am the LORD, the God of Israel, who summons you by name (Isa. 45:3).

Why does God hide the truth? So that our search will lead us to Him. A list of beliefs we could deal with, we could manage. A guide book or set of instructions we could ignore. But the person of Truth is another thing. For Truth is a person: Jesus Christ.

And let's be honest: Jesus in person makes us nervous—which is why we try to soften Him and make Him more marketable. We want people to like Jesus; we want Him to fit in, just like we want to fit in. The novelist Gail Godwin warned wryly, "Beware of ever finding a God who is totally congenial to you."[2]

When I have trouble with the Truth, it is I who needs to change, not Jesus or His Word. Who is transformed, according to Romans 12:2? We are. We are transformed by the truth, not the truth by us. "Every Christian is either a 'conformer' or a 'transformer,'" writes theologian Warren Wiersbe. "We are either fashioning our lives by pressure from without, or we are transforming our lives by power from within."[3] That power within is Jesus Christ Himself, constantly making us more and more different from the world using the instrument of truth. By focusing His gaze on our lives, He uncovers, convicts, corrects, instructs, rebukes, restores, frees, and empowers. And yes, the process makes us squirm.

"All scripture is God-breathed," Paul instructed the young pastor Timothy, "and is useful for teaching, rebuking, correcting and training in righteousness, so that the man of God may be thoroughly equipped for every good work" (2 Tim. 3:16–17).

How do I know the sky is blue, the grass is green, the earth is round, the stovetop is hot? I was taught these things. Later, I learned that $2 + 2 = 4$, that $e = mc^2$, that H_2O is the chemical formula for water, and that gravity is what holds us on the earth. Because I grew up in the United States, I was taught that all men are created equal and are entitled to certain inalienable rights—namely life, liberty, and the pursuit of happiness. Because I grew up in the sixties and seventies, I was taught that women should have equal rights with men to vote, to hold office, and to pursue an education and career. I remember how surprised I was to find that children in other countries and times were not taught these same things.

Because I grew up in the church, I was taught that Jesus loves me—a statement I accepted as equally factual. I remember how surprised I was to learn that all children were not taught this. As an adult I realize how profoundly it has affected my relationships, choices, and self-esteem, especially when I meet others who are struggling without this important piece of truth. "These commandments that I give you today are to be upon your hearts," Moses instructed the Israelites. "Impress them on your children. Talk about them when you sit at home and when you walk along the road, when you lie down and when you get up. Tie them as symbols on your hands and bind them on your foreheads. Write them on the doorframes of your houses and on your gates" (Deut. 6:6–9). Moses understood that the nation of Israel would encounter many other systems of belief on their pilgrimage to the Promised Land. The only way to preserve the truth was to be sure it was taught diligently. The truth would set them apart.

"Are you not in error because you do not know the Scriptures or the power of God?" Jesus challenged the Sadducees (Mark 12:24). It's amazing how many Christians do not know the Scriptures. I venture to say that most of us know more hymn lyrics than we know actual Scripture. Without this information, we are woefully unprepared—not only for daily life, but also to counter the variety of "truths" offered to us by the world.

Do you know what you believe, and can you find it in the Bible? Are you sure that what you believe is, in fact, in the Bible? Be careful when you speak for God that you speak His Word, not just "inspirational thoughts." You know what "inspirational thoughts" are. They sound nice, and they make great posters. My favorite example is, "If you love something, set it free. If it doesn't come back to you, it was never really yours." By the way, that's not in the Bible. What is in the Bible is, "The greatest way to show love for friends is to die for them" (John 15:13 CEV). Cross-stitch that!

Warm thoughts are nice. Positive thinking may be helpful, but it has no power. There is a difference between reading a "daily devotional" and digging into Scripture. God's Word is so powerful that some of us have been living for years off a handful of verses we learned in Vacation Bible School. Imagine how it would help to learn some new ones! And since the truth is such a powerful and incisive instrument, we must be careful to handle it accurately (2 Tim. 2:15). We must be careful that what we are learning and living is in fact God's truth, not just our version of it.

When I was growing up in the state of Texas, mixed bathing (boys and girls swimming together) was not allowed. At church camp the boys would swim from 2:00 to 3:00 and the girls would swim from 3:00 to 4:00. Imagine our surprise when our youth group went on a mission trip to Florida, and the host church threw a co-ed beach party in our honor! Apparently, mixed bathing was a regional sin.

Jesus rebuked the Pharisees for this kind of muddying of the waters:

The Pharisees and some of the teachers of the law who had come from Jerusalem gathered around Jesus and saw some of his disciples eating food with hands that were "unclean," that is, unwashed. (The Pharisees and all the Jews do not eat unless they give their hands a ceremonial washing, holding to the tradition of the elders. When they come from the marketplace, they do not eat unless they wash. And they observe many other traditions, such as the washing of cups, pitchers and kettles.)

So the Pharisees and teachers of the law asked Jesus, "Why don't your disciples live according to the tradition of the elders instead of eating their food with 'unclean' hands?"

He replied, "Isaiah was right when he prophesied about you hypocrites; as it is written: 'These people honor me with their lips, but their hearts are far from me. They worship me in vain; their teachings are but rules taught by men.' You have let go of the commands of God and are holding on to the traditions of men" (Mark 7:1–8).

When God rebukes us, He uses the truth to expose wrong thinking that leads to wrong living—because wrong living wearies us.

Then Jesus said to the crowds and to his disciples: "The teachers of the law and the Pharisees sit in Moses' seat. So you must obey them and do everything they tell you. But do not do what they do, for they do not practice what they preach. They tie up heavy loads and put them on men's shoulders, but they themselves are not willing to lift a finger to move them.

"Woe to you, teachers of the law and Pharisees, you hypocrites! You shut the kingdom of heaven in men's faces. You yourselves do not enter, nor will you let those enter who are trying to.

"Woe to you, teachers of the law and Pharisees, you hypocrites! You travel over land and sea to win a single convert, and when he becomes one, you make him twice as much a son of hell as you are" (Matt. 23:1–4,13–15).

"His commands are not burdensome," says 1 John 5:3. We will indeed grow very weary if we substitute tradition for truth. God's Word is not a list of dos and don'ts. "The words I have spoken to you are spirit and they are life," Jesus said (John 6:63). The truth feeds us; it does not eat away at us with expectations.

It's a sure sign we have become exhausted and are no longer producing what is pleasing to God when our churches foster an environment of expectations. When we start getting out our yard-sticks to measure each other, we have lost the spirit of truth. When we become dull to God's Word and lazy in our obedience to it, the first thing we entertain ourselves with is other people's business. "We hear that some among you are idle," Paul wrote to one church. "They are not busy; they are busybodies" (2 Thess. 3:11).

Busybodies—what a descriptive word. It literally means "to waste one's labor about a thing." The tabloids and reality shows have made us into a nation of busybodies, living off the drama of other people's lives, leaving our own untended. We do the same thing in the religious world. Our churches are full of people who are tiring themselves out over things that are none of their business instead of getting busy at the work they are called to be doing— namely, devoting themselves to Jesus Christ.

"Let us throw off everything that hinders and the sin that so easily entangles," urges Hebrews 12:1, "and let us run with perseverance the race marked out for us." Let us run the race marked out for us. It is wearisome to run the race marked out for another; God has neither called nor equipped us for that race— only for the race set before us.

"What about Mary?" Martha fretted. "Martha, Martha," the Lord answered, "you are worried and upset about many things, but only one thing is needed" (Luke 10:41–42).

"What about John?" Peter asked, uncomfortable under the penetrating gaze of Jesus (John 21). "What is that to you?" Jesus replied. "You follow Me."

If we breathe the air of expectations long enough, our spirits become judgmental. (That's judge-mental, as in "you must be mental if you think you are qualified to judge.") It's a short hop from judgmental to hostile and confrontational.

> Not long before it was time for Jesus to be taken up to heaven, he made up his mind to go to Jerusalem. He sent some messengers on ahead to a Samaritan village to get things ready for him. But . . . the people there refused to welcome him. When the disciples James and John saw what was happening, they asked, "Lord, do you want us to call down fire from heaven to destroy these people?" But Jesus turned and corrected them for what they had said, and said, "Don't you know what spirit you belong to? The Son of Man did not come to destroy people's lives, but to save them" (Luke 9:51–55 CEV).

Shamefully, the church today is in need of the same correction that James and John received. We are too often in fight mode, like these two brothers. "Want us to teach them a lesson for you, God? We can take 'em." The church has become more widely known for what it is against than for what it is about. We have gotten ourselves "all out of whack," as a friend of mine says, and it is the truth that corrects us.

The word *correct* means "to set straight" or "to set upright on." When we allow ourselves to become fatigued to the point that we lose perspective and fall out of step with God's Spirit, God sets us upright upon the solid foundation of His Word. "He lifted me out of the slimy pit, out of the mud and mire; he set my feet on a rock and gave me a firm place to stand," David testified in Psalm 40:2. Remember the old movies where someone would be caught in quicksand, unable to pull his feet loose, and his very struggle would cause him to sink lower and lower? That's the image of you and me, mired in the mess that is wearing us out and sucking us farther down. Like David, we need to cry out for correction: "Answer me quickly, O LORD; my spirit fails. Do not hide your face from me or I will be like those who go down to the pit. Teach me to do your will, for you are my God; may your good Spirit lead me on level ground" (Psalm 143:7, 10).

But there is good news: The truth that sets us apart, also sets us free (John 8:32). "I will walk about in freedom," declares Psalm 119:45, "for I have sought out your precepts." Perhaps we need to go back into the history of Israel to understand why this is something to sing about.

In the year 605 B.C., Babylon invaded Israel, destroyed the temple, and carried the people into slavery for 70 years. The city of Jerusalem and the temple itself lay in ruins during this time. There was no place to worship God, no place to seek forgiveness, no one to teach the Word of God. It was perhaps the darkest period in the nation's history, for God had made it clear to them they had brought this destruction upon themselves through their disobedience to His laws. The Old Testament books of Ezra and Nehemiah record the return of a Jewish remnant to Jerusalem, where they rebuilt the temple and the walls of the city. At the completion of this task the people gathered together and Ezra brought out the books of the Law. "He read it aloud from daybreak till noon," reported Nehemiah. "And all the people listened attentively to the Book of the Law" (Neh. 8:3).

> Ezra opened the book. All the people could see him because he was standing above them; and as he opened it, the people all stood up. Ezra praised the LORD, the great God; and all the people lifted their hands and responded, "Amen! Amen!" Then they bowed down and worshipped the LORD with their faces to the ground (Neh. 8:5–6).

When was the last time your congregation stood for six or more hours in rapt attention while the Scriptures were read? When have you been so hungry to hear God's Word that you cried out for it? Imagine the congregation chanting as your pastor opens the Bible: "Truth! Truth!" (which is what "Amen! Amen!" means). Have your church members ever fallen to their faces on the ground and wept in response to God's Word?

> Then Nehemiah the governor, Ezra the priest and scribe, and the Levites who were instructing the people said to them all, "This day is sacred to the LORD your God. Do not mourn or weep." For all the people had been weeping as they listened to the words of the Law.
>
> Nehemiah said, "Go and enjoy choice food and sweet drinks, and send some to those who have nothing prepared. This day is sacred to our Lord. Do not grieve, for the joy of the LORD is your strength."
>
> The Levites calmed all the people, saying, "Be still, for this is a sacred day. Do not grieve."
>
> Then all the people went away to eat and drink,

to send portions of food and to celebrate with great
joy, because they now understood the words that had
been made known to them (Neh. 8:9–12).

We who handle the Word with easy access and casual familiarity
have forgotten what good news it really is. The truth sets us free
from the burden of performance, for we have the unconditional
love of God, who chose to love us "while we were still sinners"
(Rom. 5:8).

The truth sets us free from false standards of beauty, for "the
LORD does not look at the things man looks at. Man looks at the
outward appearance, but the LORD looks at the heart" (1 Sam.
16:7).

The truth sets us free from debt and spending. "The pagans run
after all these things, and your heavenly Father knows that you
need them. But seek first his kingdom and his righteousness, and
all these things will be given to you as well" (Matt. 6:32–33).

The truth sets us free from the shame of past failures. "If we
confess our sins, he is faithful and just and will forgive us our sins
and purify us from all unrighteousness" (1 John 1:9).

The truth is the source of our spiritual birth.

- He chose to give us birth through the word of truth, that
  we might be a kind of firstfruits of all he created (James
  1:18).
- For you have been born again, not of perishable seed, but
  of imperishable, through the living and enduring word of
  God (1 Peter 1:23).

The truth trains us, growing us up the way a parent trains a child.

- Your statutes are my delight; they are my counselors (Psalm
  119:24).

🌢 Like newborn babies, crave pure spiritual milk, so that by it you may grow up in your salvation (1 Peter 2:2).

🌢 We have much to say about this, but it is hard to explain because you are slow to learn. In fact, though by this time you ought to be teachers, you need someone to teach you the elementary truths of God's word all over again. You need milk, not solid food! Anyone who lives on milk, being still an infant, is not acquainted with the teaching about righteousness. But solid food is for the mature, who by constant use have trained themselves to distinguish good from evil (Heb. 5:11–14).

When my children were small, the hardest thing to do was to take them shopping. They would tire quickly and become cranky. I could get very little done with them along. Jesus invited us to come with childlike faith, not childish faith. If I am childish in my faith, if I refuse to be trained, I will grow weary trying to keep pace with Christ. "When I was a child, I talked like a child," Paul wrote (1 Cor. 13:11). "I thought like a child, I reasoned like a child. When I became a man, I put childish ways behind me."

Following Christ requires spiritual growth to mature faith. Otherwise Christ can get nothing done with us. Our aim as disciples is that we "become mature, attaining to the whole measure of the fullness of Christ. Then we will no longer be infants, tossed back and forth by the waves, and blown here and there by every wind of teaching and by the cunning and craftiness of men in their deceitful scheming. Instead, speaking the truth in love, we will in all things grow up into him who is the Head, that is, Christ" (Eph. 4:13–15).

Truth also equips us for this new life. The Word is the sword of the Spirit in spiritual battle (Eph. 6:17). In the desert, Jesus relied on Scriptures young Hebrew boys memorized in the synagogue in order to rebuke the devil's temptations (Luke 4:1–14).

For though we live in the world, we do not wage war as the world does. The weapons we fight with are not the weapons of the world. On the contrary, they have divine power to demolish strongholds. We demolish arguments and every pretension that sets itself up against the knowledge of God, and we take captive every thought to make it obedient to Christ.

For our struggle is not against flesh and blood, but against the rulers, against the authorities, against the powers of this dark world and against the spiritual forces of evil in the heavenly realms. Therefore put on the full armor of God, so that when the day of evil comes, you may be able to stand your ground, and after you have done everything, to stand. (2 Cor. 10:3–5; Eph. 6:12–13)

Are you ready for that fight? Not until you have strapped on the belt of truth and you are ready to wield the Word of God as your sword.

Truth gives us the ability to witness. "You will be brought before kings and governors, and all on account of my name. This will result in your being witnesses to them. But make up your mind not to worry beforehand how you will defend yourselves. For I will give you words and wisdom that none of your adversaries will be able to resist or contradict" (Luke 21:12–15). "You alone have the words that impart eternal life" (John 6:68).

Truth keeps us from sin. "I have hidden your word in my heart that I might not sin against you" (Psalm 119:11). "Turn my eyes away from worthless things; preserve my life according to your word" (Psalm 119:37).

Truth strengthens us. "My soul is weary with sorrow; strengthen me according to your word" (Psalm 119:28).

Truth guides us. "Your commands make me wiser than my

enemies, for they are ever with me" (Psalm 119:98). "Your word is a lamp to my feet and a light for my path" (Psalm 119:105). "Whether you turn to the right or to the left, your ears will hear a voice behind you, saying, 'This is the way; walk in it'" (Isa. 30:21). I've often quoted this verse in a conference, only to be asked later, "How exactly does that work? How do you hear Him?" My answer is: go to the Word with a hearing heart and the intent to obey, and listen. And listen. And listen. And keep listening until you have heard Him clearly say, "This is the way."

We're not left on our own in this endeavor. "I'm going to send you a Helper," Jesus promised. "The Spirit will guide you into all truth. He will remind you of what I have said" (John 16:13; 14:26, my paraphrases).

"One of the passions I feel about women, and I feel from women, is they desire an intimacy with God, and they don't have any idea how to get it," says speaker and author Esther Burroughs. "They run from retreat to retreat and seminar to seminar. They're groupies, and they follow speakers." What we're looking for, Esther says, is a woman with an underlined Bible to tell us what she has heard from God, when we have the same Bible and the same Spirit at work in us. The sad result is that "[we] give away a power to the speaker that is available to every single one of us: the power that comes from knowing God intimately."[4] Because we have the Holy Spirit living in us, every believer can read and understand God's Word, can hear Him speak to us personally, and can live in relationship with Him. Do not take this privilege lightly; it was bought for us at the price of Jesus Christ's death.

God goes out of His way to meet those who are thirsty for truth. The Apostle John pointed this out in his account of Jesus' encounter with the woman at the well (John 4). John began to tell this story with the words "Now he had to go through Samaria."

No, He didn't.

As a matter of fact, no self-respecting Jew of that time would go through Samaria. The Samaritans were a mixed race, part Jew and part Gentile, a result of their Assyrian captivity. Their little wedge of a province lay right in the middle of Palestine. In order to travel from Judea (the southern province) up to Galilee (the northern province), the Jews went an extra distance east across the Jordan River and through the barren wilderness of Perea just to avoid even stepping in Samaria. This is the route Jesus would have taken—except, as John wryly commented, "He had to go through Samaria."

Why? Because a woman would be all alone at a well at midday (an unlikely hour)—a woman so thirsty for love she had been through five husbands of her own and who-knows-how-many others. A scandalous woman, so weary of being an outcast that she went to the well in the heat of the day to avoid the jibes and stares of other women. A seeker who knew the prophecies and longed to find the truth. To this unlikely candidate, the Truth chose to reveal Himself. She was the first person to whom Jesus said, "I AM the Messiah." "He knew everything about me," the woman declared. And this was good news.

"The LORD is near to all who call on Him in truth," Psalm 145:18 assures us. "The LORD confides in those who fear him; he makes his covenant known to them" (Psalm 25:14). "So I say to you: Ask and it will be given to you; seek and you will find; knock and the door will be opened to you. For everyone who asks receives; he who seeks finds; and to him who knocks, the door will be opened" (Luke 11:9–10).

You have His Word on that.

CHAPTER 6

Growing Weary Without Abiding

I am the vine, you are the branches; he who abides in Me, and I in him, he bears much fruit; for apart from Me, you can do nothing.
—John 15:5 NASB

You and I are what we are when we are alone [with Jesus]. Talk with Him, listen to Him, look at Him.
—Corrie ten Boom[1]

I sit down for a half hour early each morning to write all the things I hope to do that day, letting myself believe I can do it all," artist Sue Bender told news anchor Peter Jennings.

Bender continued, "There's a connection between my lists and the piles of paper that cover every usable surface in my room. The piles are winning the war, I told my friend Yvonne one day. No matter how hard I work, I don't seem to make a dent in them. I tell her emphatically, this is a metaphor for my life. And she replied, 'It's not a *metaphor* for your life, this *is* your life.' "[2]

What is your life? Papers, diapers, numbers, figures, flow charts, flip charts, sweat socks, declining stocks? Do you make lists and piles, separating your life like laundry? Friends over here, family over there. Details over here, God over there. This I can handle; this, I need help. Life is one great big pie chart, and God is a wedge.

Oswald Chambers wrote about this in *My Utmost for His Highest*. Explaining why Abram pitched his tent and built an altar between the cities of Bethel and Ai (see Genesis 12:8), he wrote:

> Bethel is the symbol of fellowship with God; Ai is the symbol of the world. Abram "pitched his tent" between the two. The lasting value of our public service for God is measured by the depth of the intimacy of our private times of fellowship and oneness with Him . . . . That is why we must "pitch our tents" where we will always have quiet times with Him, however noisy our times with the world may be. There are not three levels of spiritual life—worship, waiting and work. Yet some of us seem to jump like spiritual frogs from worship to waiting, and from waiting to work. God's idea is that the three should go together.[3]

Jesus likened this way of life to a vine and its branches. The grapevines that covered the hills of Palestine were abundantly productive. They grew from roots as thick as a man's arm. They drew their nourishment, their life, through these roots. A branch broken off from the vine would shrivel and die. "In the same way," Jesus said, "your life is in Me. Apart from Me you can produce nothing." Nothing.

This was exactly the relationship Jesus said He had with His Father. "By myself I can do nothing," He said, "for I seek not to please myself but him who sent me" (John 5:30). Jesus Himself was concerned with producing what was pleasing and beautiful to His Father; and even He could not do this on His own.

What is abiding? To abide is to pray, wait, depend. It is to let go of things we cannot control (which is everything) and to hold on to God's capable hand. It is to dwell in—to inhabit—the land of daily routine and relationships, knowing that God is present and active there. It is tending soil, pruning, and weeding. It is letting our roots go down deep. It is taking baby steps. Abiding is not what we do in between life; abiding is life.

"In him we live and move and have our being," Paul said (Acts 17:28). Abiding is breathing in and breathing out the air of God's Spirit and putting one foot in front of the other every day, just as we did the day before and the day before that. The Life inside makes the life outside possible.

"The acid test of Christianity is not giving our life at the stake or in the lion's den," writes Jean Fleming, "but giving it little by little, day after day, moment by moment, a drop at a time, in the common duties of life assigned to us." [4]

"The problem with abiding," my friend says, "is that it does not feel very productive."

This is because we do not know the true meaning of the word *productive*. We define productive as "busy." We wrongly assume that the busiest person is the most productive person, the most valuable player, the one that gets results. How many reports can you churn out? How many loads of laundry can you wash and fold? Results have become our measuring stick, and we wear ourselves out trying to "wow" people with our numbers, our packaging, our market share, the size of our waist, or the shine on our floor—only to feel the burden of trying to top these standards the next time.

The church has come to feel this pressure, too. Every week exhausted, bleary-eyed people drag themselves into our pews and demand that we dazzle them enough that they will come back next week. A relationship with God has become a weekend getaway, rather than what it was intended to be: life itself.

If the Spirit addressed the mainstream church in America today, I believe His message would be very close to the one found in Revelation 3:14–18. The Laodiceans were so prosperous, their culture so materially productive, they did not even recognize their poverty of spirit.

"Blessed are the poor in spirit," Jesus taught. In other words, blessed are those who know they are spiritually needy (Matt. 5:3). God is fully present with those who recognize that they need Him. "I will cry out to God who accomplishes all things for me," David sang (Psalm 57:2 NASB). "He gives strength to the weary and increases the power of the weak," says Isaiah 40:29.

Conversely, not blessed are those who are not poor in spirit. If blessed means "filled with God's presence," then those who do not admit inadequacy do not have the benefits of His presence. "You do not have, because you do not ask God," James exhorted (4:2).

"In repentance and rest is your salvation, in quietness and trust is your strength, but you would have none of it," Isaiah rebuked the kingdom of Judah. "You said, 'No, we will flee on horses.' Therefore you will flee! You said, 'We will ride off on swift horses.' Therefore your pursuers will be swift! . . . Yet the LORD longs to be gracious to you; he rises to show you compassion. For the LORD is a God of justice. Blessed are all who wait for him!" (Isa. 30:15–18).

A great deal of abiding in Christ is asking and waiting. We don't do either very well, and I think that's because both asking and waiting require us to acknowledge that we are not in control. We are not quite convinced that God will come through for us in the manner we want—and we are certain He won't answer on our timetable. So we waste a lot of time and energy checking up on God, making sure He did get our memo and has gone right to work on it. Second-guessing God wears us out.

"For I am confident of this very thing, that He who began a good work in you will perfect it until the day of Christ Jesus" (Phil. 1:6 NASB). Paul wrote these words to a group of believers who were past the initial rush of evangelism and church-starting. Facing the realities of church order, the influence of pagan culture, and Paul's imprisonment, the fervor was beginning to subside. Pessimism had set in. It's exciting to trust God as He does a powerful new work. But then comes that stretch of time in which there are no fireworks, no great displays of the supernatural, just steady, persistent plodding required. Be assured, Paul said, that He never starts anything He does not finish. "So then, my beloved . . . work out your salvation with fear and trembling, for it is God who is at work in you" (Phil. 2:12–13 NASB). Those who abide know that God is at work, even when we don't see it.

Imagine yourself as one of Jesus' first disciples. Just two days ago you made the momentous decision to leave everything behind to follow the Messiah. "But first," He said, "we need to stop at my cousin's wedding."

Two important background notes: First, some of these men were formerly followers of John the Baptist—most likely members of the Essenes, a Jewish sect who practiced an ascetic lifestyle in the wilderness at Qumran. They were used to living in caves and eating bugs. Second, a wedding in Jesus' time was not a 30-minute ceremony with reception afterward in the fellowship hall. It was party-hearty: revelry, dancing, eating, and drinking for days. This is where Jesus made His first stop with His new followers. They must have wondered what they'd gotten themselves into—it was all so indulgent and so . . . well, ordinary!

Never assume just because the situation is ordinary that God is not doing something extraordinary. Jesus' first miracle in Cana was a private lesson for His disciples' benefit. Only John recorded the event, because he was there (John 2:1–11). Author Philip Yancey suggests that the water that became wine was taken from the urns of ceremonial water used for foot-washing. Jesus symbolically demonstrated that the old cleansing rituals were about to be replaced by the only true purifying agent: His blood. But He also taught His new disciples an important truth: God hangs out in ordinary places. In practical ways, He reveals himself and demonstrates His power to those who look for Him in everyday life.

"Trust in the Lord, and do good," Psalm 37 says. "Dwell in the land and cultivate faithfulness" (v. 3 NASB). The word *trust* here means "to rely on for safety or security." Psalm 63:8 describes this kind of trust: "My soul clings to you." The word *dwell* means "to settle down, abide, inhabit." These were odd instructions to a nation who had left the slavery of Egypt to wander in the wilderness for a generation, constantly making camp, then packing up and moving on. We should be able to relate to that. We live in a restless society; we are constantly moving on—up the career ladder, to a bigger house, the next project, the newest car, the latest entertainment.

Put down roots, God says. Settle in. Make a life for yourself. Get to know your neighbors. Drive a carpool. Serve on committees. Plant a garden. Go to the office. Do the daily routine—only do these things as one who is clinging to God. Don't wait until things settle down to have time for Him. God does not wait for you to get to a certain place in your life before He gets involved. He is at work in you and around you even when you think you've been sidetracked.

> Now Moses was tending the flock of Jethro . . . and he led the flock to the far side of the desert and came to Horeb. . . . The angel of the LORD appeared to him in flames of fire from within a bush . . . .
>
> The LORD said, "I have indeed seen the misery of my people in Egypt . . . . So I have come down to rescue them . . . . I am sending you to Pharaoh to bring my people . . . out of Egypt" (Ex. 3:1–10).

God had carefully positioned Moses to deliver Israel—so carefully that Moses was even raised in the house of Pharaoh. However, at a key moment, Moses failed and ran as far as he could get from Egypt (Ex. 3). He was "sent down to the minors" to tend sheep instead of shepherd a nation. But as many of us have discovered, God goes behind, beside, and before us, and sometimes He goes out of His way. On this particular day He had to go clear to the far side of the desert of Midian to meet with Moses. Just to be sure He got Moses' attention, He set a bush on fire.

"I have come down to rescue the Israelites," God said. Where had God descended from? Heaven! God told Moses His name, "I AM." God is the source of everything, the One who can do anything. He had all the resources of heaven and earth at His disposal, but He chose to use Moses' forty years of experience at tending sheep in the desert. I'll bet Moses thought he was wasting his time all those years!

"We do not know today whether we are busy or idle," wrote Ralph Waldo Emerson. "In times when we thought ourselves indolent, we have afterwards discovered that much was accomplished and much was begun in us."[5]

Those who abide know that nothing in our lives is ever wasted.

As Jesus began His public ministry, He sought out four men— Peter, Andrew, James, and John—and found them, skilled fishermen, hard at their work. All four were typical Galilean men of their time: strong-willed, passionate, bold. Andrew's first impulse upon meeting Christ was to introduce Him to his brother Peter; he was a natural evangelist (John 1:41). Christ called them to put their skill and passion to work for a greater purpose: fishing for men.

Must a fisherman stop being a fisherman to become a witness? No. God does not call us to give up who we are, but to consecrate who we are to Him. The missionaries and missions volunteers I meet prepared for a career about which they are passionate: teaching, medicine, agriculture, media, sports, home-making. Along the way, God called them to a greater passion: winning people to Christ. Then He employed the skills, training, and experience of their life's work toward this new purpose.

A friend told me about her efforts to decide which college she should attend. Which was God's plan? What if she chose the wrong one? A wise counselor told her, "Eve, no matter which place you choose, God will be there."

"'Am I only a God nearby,' declared the LORD, 'and not a God far away? Do I not fill heaven and earth?' declared the LORD" (Jer. 23:23–24). What a relief to know there is no Door #1, #2 or #3, that we do not have to guess behind which door God hides. Wherever we go, He is there before us, beside us, and behind us. God is always at work around us.

My grandfather, B. B. Cox, was a Baptist preacher in Louisiana. I've heard that he was criticized by his congregation for playing dominoes with the local men on Saturday night. Some members complained because he was hanging out with the Catholics and the "heathen." Several years ago at a picnic, I met a member of my husband's family who lives in Louisiana. When I mentioned my grandfather her eyes filled with tears and she took my hand. "Oh, honey," she said, "if it weren't for your grandfather, my daddy might never have known the Lord. He witnessed to those men every Saturday night."

"The God I know does not want us to divide life up into compartments—'This part is spiritual, so this is God's province,'" Catherine Marshall wrote. "If we are to believe Jesus, His Father and our Father is the God of all life."[6] He is the God of colleges and careers, of work and play, of sacred and secular. He is even the God of dominoes.

I played with dominoes when I was a little girl. I liked to stand them on end, one behind another, in a long, snaking path. Then I would hold my breath and flick the first domino with my finger, causing the whole line to fall backward in a delightful cascade. Every domino had to be set in place just so, or the trick wouldn't work.

I need to see my life as part of a long series of events, carefully lined up by God to accomplish His purposes. Only He knows when every domino is in place. One obedient moment follows another, leading to God's final result.

Joseph did not comprehend this when his brothers sold him to passing gypsies. He did not grasp it when he was disgraced and imprisoned in Potiphar's house, nor when he was restored to favor and placed in charge of Egypt's food supplies. The Israelites did not understand this when they were later enslaved in Egypt. But Psalm 105:17 reveals God's hand: "He sent a man before them—Joseph, sold as a slave." In a time of famine, Israel became strong, educated, and well-fed, because God saw to it that Joseph was positioned at the right time and place. There are seasons when I don't understand what God is up to in my life. Well, maybe it's not about me at all. Those who abide know that they are part of a long process; the timing is up to God. We have offered our lives for His purpose.

"I planted the seed, Apollos watered it, but God made it grow," Paul said. "So neither he who plants nor he who waters is anything, but only God, who makes things grow. The man who plants and the man who waters have one purpose, and each will be rewarded according to his own labor" (1 Cor. 3:6–8).

Sometimes our job is simply to prepare the way: to plant seeds and till the soil, preparing hearts for the moment when Christ will reveal Himself. John the Baptist was not the Messiah and he knew it. His role was to prepare the hearts of the people to receive the Christ. From him we can learn some things about the ministry of preparing the way. It calls for boldness and passion. Isaiah likened it to leveling mountains and redirecting roadways. It likely requires going "where no one has gone before." It also requires letting go. The one who calls people to repentance will probably not have the ministry of discipling them. After you've gotten in their faces, they aren't comfortable to have you walk along beside! There is a moment when the work must be handed off. Just as surely as you must be certain of the call to prepare the way, you must be ready for the moment to yield the way. John in fact anointed Christ as the One to follow. "He must increase, but I must decrease," he said (John 3:30 NASB).

Some of the most passionate Christian workers I know have burned out because they did not recognize or accept the moment to let go. "And by the seventh day God completed His work which He had done; and He rested," says the account of Creation (Gen. 2:2 NASB). Somewhere we've gotten the idea that God never says, "Done." This is part of our American work ethic. We don't know when to quit. But God does.

"The hour has come . . . I have finished the work You gave me to do," Jesus pronounced (John 17:1,4 TEV). There is a time for everything, which implies there is a time when one thing is done and another is begun. God, who started the work, knows when each task is completed; but often we don't listen when He says, "Time to move on." For us to keep tinkering away is to say, "That's not enough." If God says, "Done," then put your tools away; He is God. Rest is a reward enjoyed by those who trust God's timetable.

"He has made everything beautiful in its time," wrote Solomon. "He has also set eternity in the hearts of men; yet they cannot fathom what God has done from beginning to end" (Eccl. 3:11). Why doesn't God tell us what He's up to? "Why are there times when I don't know, and it doesn't seem to matter," muses Sue Bender, "and times when not knowing fills me with dread?"[7]

"God doesn't give blueprints to any of us for the entire span of life ahead," writes Edith Schaeffer. "This is one of the things concerning prayer that causes me to realize day by day, and year after year in my own life, that God has given something very priceless in not giving blueprints and in not giving outlined answers that cover a long time ahead. He has kept us and keeps us now in a position in which we need that communication day after day to know one step at a time."[8]

Schaeffer points to Isaiah 50:10–11, words that have influenced decisions regarding her work and life: "Who among you fears the LORD and obeys the word of his servant? Let him who walks in the dark, who has no light, trust in the name of the LORD and rely on his God. But now, all you who light fires and provide yourselves with flaming torches, go, walk in the light of your fires and of the torches you have set ablaze. This is what you shall receive from my hand: You will lie down in torment." Shaeffer continued:

> It is a warning to watch out for impatience in wanting to "get on with it," whatever "it" happens to be. God tells us that to be in a fog, a dark place, to have no clue of what comes next, is to be in a place where we need to trust Him and keep our hand in His hand, waiting for Him to show us where to go or what to do next . . . .
>
> We are where we are today, each of us. You are a doctor today in one particular town, or you are a bookstore seller today; you are a dentist today, or you are a grocer at this time; you are a grandmother to-day. Today you and I are involved in a great number of things, fulfilling the purposes for which God has us where we are, doing the combination of routine or imaginative things we are doing. All right—you and I often want to know, "What comes next?" God is saying, "Trust Me." He is saying, "Stay in the place where you are until I show you . . . what comes next." He is saying, "Blessed is the person who waits in the dark, holding My hand."[9]

My friend tells me, "I feel that God is asking me to get prepared for something. I don't know what it is, and I don't think I want to know." Yes. I'm pretty sure one of the reasons God doesn't show us the future is that we would run away screaming. We are not yet where we need to be to accept that piece of information. We are not ready.

We run ahead of God when we refuse to wait on Him to prepare us. We need to be taught, trained, even disciplined.

You have forgotten that word of encouragement that addresses you as sons: "My son, do not make light of the Lord's discipline, and do not lose heart when he rebukes you, because the Lord disciplines those he loves, and he punishes everyone he accepts as a son." Our fathers disciplined us for a little while as they thought best; but God disciplines us for our good, that we may share in his holiness. No discipline seems pleasant at the time, but painful. Later on, however, it produces a harvest of righteousness and peace for those who have been trained by it. Therefore, strengthen your feeble arms and weak knees. Make level paths for your feet, so that the lame may not be disabled, but rather healed (Heb. 12:5–6,10–13).

"There are no shortcuts to anyplace worth going," said the great soprano Beverly Sills. Satan offered Jesus a shortcut: "The devil led him up to a high place and showed him in an instant all the kingdoms of the world. And he said to him, 'I will give you all their authority and splendor, for it has been given to me, and I can give it to anyone I want to. So if you worship me, it will all be yours'" (Luke 4:5–7). Imagine if Jesus had taken that shortcut.

Jesus repeatedly resisted His followers' urgings to "get on with it." "It's not time yet," He often replied. Jesus was moving on God's timetable, waiting for the necessary preparations, doing what He was given to do in the meantime, and often withdrawing to be with God. When Jesus urged, "Come away and rest," or chose to stop for lunch with someone, the disciples were not always patient. But when Jesus finally said, "The time has come," when the crucial hour came for the will of God to be done, Jesus moved almost in fast-forward, while the disciples were too tired to keep up.

He took Peter and the two sons of Zebedee along with him, and he began to be sorrowful and troubled. Then he said to them, "My soul is overwhelmed with sorrow to the point of death. Stay here and keep watch with me." Going a little farther, he fell with his face to the ground and prayed, "My Father, if it is possible, may this cup be taken from me. Yet not as I will, but as you will." Then he returned to his disciples and found them sleeping. "Could you men not keep watch with me for one hour?" he asked Peter. "Watch and pray so that you will not fall into temptation. The spirit is willing, but the body is weak" (Matt. 26:37–41).

When we exhaust ourselves straining at God's timetable, when we refuse opportunities to rest and prepare, we meet the moment undersupplied. This is a great opportunity for Satan. Too tired to pray? Then you have no wisdom or power. The body is weak; it is easily discouraged, depleted, overcome. But the Spirit knows how to prepare us for the moment. He paces us so that we are instructed, trained, experienced, and rested. He does not lead us into the moment of confrontation so exhausted that we can't stay awake.

Abiding means accepting that I am a human being with physical limitations. I must live within the guidelines God has given me. I must rest. I must eat right. I must work hard, and I must know when to stop. This is difficult for me. But God set those limitations for my protection. Christians should be the healthiest humans alive. When I ignore my physical well-being, I buck the Creator Himself.

We run ahead of God when we go out without His authority. "Unless the LORD builds the house, its builders labor in vain," says Psalm 127:1.

Matthew 10 gives us the account of Jesus sending out His disciples on His behalf for the first time. "He called his twelve disciples to him and gave them authority to drive out evil spirits and to heal every disease and sickness" (v. 1). He also gave them specific instructions about how, when, and where to go. And He gave them the power to do these tasks. Before Jesus issued His Great Commission to His disciples, He first established, "All authority in heaven and on earth has been given to me. Therefore go" (Matt. 28:18–19). Again, He gave them specific instructions for what to do. Luke recorded, "On one occasion, while he was eating with them, he gave them this command: 'Do not leave Jerusalem, but wait for the gift my Father promised, which you have heard me speak about. For John baptized with water, but in a few days you will be baptized with the Holy Spirit'" (Acts 1:4–5). "You will receive power when the Holy Spirit comes on you," Jesus instructed, and you will be My witnesses.

The Spirit gifts believers as He wills (1 Cor. 12:11). When He calls us to a work, He equips us for that work. God also withholds spiritual gifts as purposefully as He distributes them. Tools we don't need are useless for the job. So is a worker who has not been instructed in his task. The surest way to wear yourself out is to jump into a work for which the Spirit has not equipped you, nor the Lord instructed you. "But I am good at this," you say. "I did it in my old church." Maybe so, but you'd better not appoint yourself to do it in this situation, or you'll wind up with a mess of trouble.

God places us within His body of believers, a body with many parts, but only one Head. God designed us to work within a body, so that everyone has a function, an appointed task. The eye cannot say, "I want to be a hand this week." The ear cannot say, "I'm so good at hearing, I'd probably be good at smelling, too." An ear makes a lousy nose. To usurp the authority of the Creator is to injure the body, endanger yourself, and guarantee a malfunction. Abiding means being what God created you to be and functioning in the role in which He places you.

God also places us within His body of believers so that we will not be left without help and protection. "Two are better than one, because they have a good return for their work," says Ecclesiastes 4:9–12. "If one falls down, his friend can help him up. But pity the man who falls and has no one to help him up! Also, if two lie down together, they will keep warm. But how can one keep warm alone? Though one may be overpowered, two can defend themselves. A cord of three strands is not quickly broken." That cord of three strands is I, my brother—or sister—believer, and Christ. We dare not go out without them at our side. "Let us consider how we may spur one another on toward love and good deeds," urges Hebrews 10:24–25. "Let us not give up meeting together, as some are in the habit of doing, but let us encourage one another—and all the more as you see the Day approaching."

The word *encourage* means "to cover with your heart." When I am most discouraged and weary, my first response is to pick up the phone and say, "Cover me." I have a list of people I can ask, but there are a handful of friends without whose covering I would never attempt anything: Kim, Saralu, Mike, Jolene, Monica, Alice Ruth. I hope you have a handful of names of your own. And I hope you realize the power of intercession and accountability.

"Is any one of you sick?" asked James, the leader of the church in Jerusalem. "He should call the elders of the church to pray over him and anoint him with oil in the name of the Lord." The condition referred to here is "sick from sinning"—it is spiritual sickness. "And the prayer offered in faith will make the sick person well; the Lord will raise him up. If he has sinned, he will be forgiven. Therefore confess your sins to each other and pray for each other so that you may be healed. The prayer of a righteous man is powerful and effective" (James 5:14–16). "If anyone sees his brother commit a sin that does not lead to death, he should pray and God will give him life," instructs 1 John 5:16.

An intercessor is a mediator, a "go-between." An intercessor goes to God on my behalf, presenting my needs—those I am aware of and those I am not. An intercessor asks God to work His will in my life. An intercessor also goes to me on God's behalf, encouraging me with God's Word and sometimes speaking the message of accountability I am unwilling to hear from God. The prophet Nathan was this kind of intercessor for King David, pointing out David's sin with Bathsheba and leading him to repentance and restoration (2 Sam. 12). It is both a privilege and an awesome responsibility to be an intercessor. To pray for another is a selfless act. In a very real way, we are laying down our lives for our friends.

I want to pause here to speak my mind about something. I suspect that the great spiritual malaise that has overtaken the church is due in part to our failure to intercede for others, particularly for our brothers and sisters who do the work of missions around the world. It is boring to pray only for yourself and those with whom you have a personal connection. We need to reorient ourselves to realize that we are personally connected with our missionaries and with other Christians worldwide through the person of Jesus Christ. Their burdens are our burdens; their work is our work. The people to whom they witness are our concern. They should be our primary concern, because they are Christ's passion.

I am not making a blanket statement about all church members; I know many, many people who faithfully spend themselves in prayer for missions and missionaries, for evangelical work around the world. I am saying that when I look around and listen, I find that the preponderance of our public prayer is about getting a job or selling our house or the latest update on who's having surgery. These are legitimate concerns, but the fact that they are so enormous to us reveals that we do not understand the size and scope of God's concerns.

Our window on the world is too small. Something is seriously wrong when we find the spread of the gospel boring, when the knowledge that there are people in the world who do not know God does not cause us to hit our knees in fervent intercession. Our God is doing a great and mighty work today in parts of the world where people have never before even heard the name of Jesus Christ. Governments are being overturned. Idols are being toppled. Prisoners are being set free. Hungry people eat, and sick people receive medical treatment. Those whose lives have been crippled by ignorance and intolerance are hearing the truth for the first time, and it is good news. Oh, it is good news. Our God reigns! Sing it, shout it. Stand on the pews. Fall on your face and plead for those who carry the good news. They do your work and my work. Many of them are the only Christian witness for hundreds of miles.

In a dark place in his life, my friend Chris Wommack prayed, "Lord, tell the people who love me to pray for me." Paul constantly asked the New Testament believers to pray for him—not for safety or ease, but for boldness, that he would not grow weary.

In 1987, due to the dangerous political climate in Lebanon, the US evacuated all Americans living and working there. Several months later, Frances Fuller, former missionary to Lebanon, stood before a congregation and announced, "I am here today because you prayed the wrong prayer. You prayed for my safety. You should have prayed for me to remain bold at any cost."[10]

I admit that I am often guilty of asking for ease and safety, both for myself and those I love. "He does not promise us that everything is going to go smoothly," writes Edith Schaeffer. "The smoothness of the next step is not the criterion of your having found the Lord's will. Satan would like us to be confused on that point! May we never forget it."[11] Those who abide know that being in God's will doesn't guarantee being out of harm's way.

In fact, the deeper we go into Jesus' life, the more ability we have to face harm gracefully for His sake. Acts 4:1–30 tells of Peter and John in Jerusalem during a time of great growth for the early Christian church. Peter and John had healed a crippled man who sat every day at the Temple gate. Many had heard of the miracle and believed in Jesus as a result. The chief priests had Peter and John thrown in jail. These were the same ones who had plotted to kill Jesus, had Him arrested and taken before Pilate. Peter and John knew that they were effective if the priests wanted to get rid of someone!

The Sanhedrin interrogated Peter and John about the miracle, and the Scripture describes Peter as "filled with the Holy Spirit" when he replied. Make no mistake, Peter told them, if you are asking by what power this crippled man was healed, it is by the power of Jesus Christ, *whom you crucified.*

Pretty bold speech from a prisoner to a captive! However, the Sanhedrin could take no action because so many had witnessed the miracle. They decided to warn Peter and John to speak no more in Jesus' name. The disciples' reply was swift. "Judge for yourselves whether it is right in God's sight to obey you rather than God. For we cannot help speaking about what we have seen and heard."

When they were released, Peter and John went back to their own people and told all that the chief priests and elders had said to them. Then they prayed.

How would we have prayed if two of our members reported that they had been imprisoned and warned not to talk about Jesus? Most likely we would pray for protection. We would ask God to keep them safe.

How do you think they prayed? The believers in the church in Jerusalem sang a hymn we know as Psalm 2, a psalm written by King David, who had seen government after government oppose God and fall. Then they recounted what they personally had witnessed: the face-off between the current powers and their Master, Jesus Christ. They acknowledged the threat from the city leaders. Then they prayed: "Now, Lord, consider their threats and enable your servants to speak your word with great boldness. Stretch out your hand to heal and perform miraculous signs and wonders through the name of your holy servant Jesus" (Acts 4:29–30).

They asked for *boldness* and for *more miracles* in the name of Jesus. The first act of the believers in Jerusalem was to acknowledge who was really in charge and then to worship Him. They got their perspective straight. As a result, they prayed that God's will would be accomplished. They made a request that they knew with confidence God would answer "Yes."

"After they prayed, the place where they were meeting was shaken. And they were all filled with the Holy Spirit and spoke the word of God boldly" (Acts 4:31).

To abide is to stand firmly in a place that is shaken. To abide is to live in the eye of a mighty storm. My family experienced Hurricane Erin firsthand when it hit the coast of Florida in the summer of 1994. The storm moved in so quickly that we and other vacationers were unable to evacuate, so we hunkered down in our beach cottages and literally rode out the storm. Although very little in our community was damaged, it was breathtaking to witness the sheer power of nature as it bent great trees horizontal and lifted the ocean in twenty-five-foot walls of water. I confess that I do not pray for God's will to be done at times because I am afraid to unleash that power into my carefully constructed world. I know that things—that I—will get broken and bent. But consider Sue Bender's observation: "I saw a strikingly handsome Japanese tea bowl that had been broken and pieced together. The image of that bowl made a lasting impression. Instead of trying to hide the flaws, the cracks were emphasized—filled with silver. The bowl was even more precious after it had been mended."[12]

We grow weary trying to keep ourselves from being scarred by life, to remain unmarred. Like Mary of Bethany's alabaster vase, we are intended to be broken and spilled out. The most beautiful One of us all was broken. Paul wrote, "He said to me, 'My grace is sufficient for you, for my power is made perfect in weakness.' Therefore I will boast all the more gladly about my weaknesses, so that Christ's power may rest on me. That is why, for Christ's sake, I delight in weaknesses, in insults, in hardships, in persecutions, in difficulties. For when I am weak, then I am strong" (2 Cor. 12:9–10).

Brokenness and restoration, dying and resurrection are the pattern of our daily lives. Yet we are taken aback by this process. "Dear friends, do not be surprised at the painful trial you are suffering, as though something strange were happening to you," Peter wrote to the first-century believers. "But rejoice that you participate in the sufferings of Christ, so that you may be overjoyed when his glory is revealed. So then, those who suffer according to God's will should commit themselves to their faithful Creator and *continue to do good*" (1 Peter 4:12–13,19, italics mine). God ordains that the mission of His church move forward not only by the fuel of worship and in the power of prayer, but at the price of suffering. To abide is to place your confidence not in your circumstances, but in the One who is with you in the midst of them. "Though an army besiege me, my heart will not fear," David testified. "Though war break out against me, even then will I be confident" (Psalm 27:3).

Shadrach, Meshach, and Abednego were faced with a life-or-death choice—to worship God or to bow to a golden statue. Their decision incurred King Nebuchadnezzar's wrath and punishment (Dan. 3). "If we are thrown into the blazing furnace," Shadrach, Meshach, and Abednego reasoned, "the God we serve is able to save us from it, and he will rescue us from your hand, O king. But even if he does not, we want you to know, O king, that we will not serve your gods or worship the image of gold you have set up" (Dan. 3:17–18). Even as they spoke these words, the three could already smell the flames.

Why do we presume God wants to spare us the fire? He never promised this. He promised, "When you pass through the waters, I will be with you. . . . When you walk through the fire, you will not be burned; the flames will not set you ablaze" (Isa. 43:2). Getting burned isn't the worst thing that can happen, nor is physical death.

The worst is to be separated from God. The fiercest trial can't do that. "One thing I ask," pleaded David. "Do not hide your face from me, do not turn your servant away in anger; you have been my helper. Do not reject me or forsake me, O God my Savior" (Psalm 27:9).

Those who abide know that God lives in the eye of the storm. "Do not be afraid," God assures us, "for I am with you" (Isa. 43:5).

- This is what the LORD says: "Let not the wise man boast of his wisdom or the strong man boast of his strength or the rich man boast of his riches, but let him who boasts boast about this: that he understands and knows me, that I am the LORD, who exercises kindness, justice and righteousness on earth, for in these I delight" (Jer. 9:23–24).

- Praise the LORD, O my soul; all my inmost being, praise his holy name. Praise the LORD, O my soul, and forget not all his benefits—who forgives all your sins and heals all your diseases, who redeems your life from the pit and crowns you with love and compassion, who satisfies your desires with good things so that your youth is renewed like the eagle's (Psalm 103:1–5).

- Why are you downcast, O my soul? Why so disturbed within me? Put your hope in God, for I will yet praise him, my Savior and my God (Psalm 42:11).

- Let Israel say—if the LORD had not been on our side when men attacked us, when their anger flared against us, they would have swallowed us alive; the flood would have engulfed us, the torrent would have swept over us, the raging waters would have swept us away.

- Praise be to the LORD, who has not let us be torn by their teeth. We have escaped like a bird out of the fowler's snare; the snare has been broken, and we have escaped. Our help is in the name of the LORD, the Maker of heaven and earth (Psalm 124).

"My soul glorifies the Lord," sang a young—and pregnant—virgin named Mary, "and my spirit rejoices in God my Savior . . . for the Mighty One has done great things for me—holy is his name. His mercy extends to those who fear him, from generation to generation" (Luke 1:46–50). Paul and Silas, in a Philippian prison cell, sang praises until the walls shook and the prison doors were rattled open. The Apostle John was exiled to Patmos in order to discourage him, to shut him up; instead John had a revelation of worship that empowers believers to this day. "Patmos is the place the world sends you to forget about you," my friend and pastor Mike Glenn says. "Patmos is being out of the loop, having no influence, doing without, being cut off. But Patmos is where Jesus is waiting to meet you."

To abide is to get to know what the presence of God feels like, to recognize it, rejoice in it, take strength from it. To abide is to learn to live on a different level, to be attentive to the activity and the stillness below the surface of daily life, to know that what is being produced may yet be unseen. Abiding does not come naturally, but it is necessary. Rosalie Beck described this in an article she wrote: "'Be still and know that I am God' (Psalm 46:10) is not just a nice phrase or a helpful suggestion—it is an affirmation of critical importance. . . . For many [Christians], 'doing good things' consumes our days. We feel selfish if we take time for ourselves. Those of us who feel this way especially need time to be silent before God. Only in the quiet of God's presence will we find renewal and strength to become listening hearts. . . . Do you wish to become a listening heart? Then create silence. Be still and know God. From the knowledge of God comes the capacity to minister."[13]

A life of abiding will be a source of consternation to the world. Why aren't we worried? Why aren't we stressed? Why aren't we bustling about taking care of business? And why don't we have a plan?

People of faith do have a plan: to trust God and obey Him. "By faith Abraham, when called . . . obeyed and went, even though he did not know where he was going" (Heb. 11:8). Many people of faith have been out on that limb. I have! Looking back, I see that at every major turning point in our lives, Dennis and I only knew it was time to stop doing what we were doing. That's all God told us.

"What will you do next?" people asked.

"We don't know yet," we'd reply.

This infuriated some of our family and friends. Weren't we being irresponsible? Maybe so, if you have to know the details. But we know the One who holds the details—and us—in His hand.

Worry is the opposite of abiding. When we worry, we take on responsibility that is not ours. Jesus didn't say, "Don't tend to your everyday life." He Himself saw to people's physical needs. What He said was, "Don't worry about it." Don't take the responsibility on yourself. That's the way the world lives (Matt. 6:32–33). It is the great failing of humans to always want more. Whatever we have, it isn't enough. By contrast, God's people should be free from the rat race of maintaining a certain standard of living.

"Be content with what you have, because God has said, 'Never will I leave you; never will I forsake you'" (Heb. 13:5). The abundant life Jesus described is not up to us to procure. When we surrender the role of provider, we have more. We have rest, peace, joy, love for others, generosity, time. All these are supplied by the One who is able "to do immeasurably more than all we ask or imagine" (Eph. 3:20–21). Peter told us we have everything we need for life (material needs) and godliness (spiritual needs) in Jesus Christ (2 Pet. 1:3).

"Everything is already yours as a gift," Paul wrote, "all of it is yours, and you are privileged to be in union with Christ, who is in union with God" (1 Cor. 3:21–23 *The Message*). Christ doesn't give us something we can take for our weariness; He gives us Himself. "He himself is our peace," says Ephesians 2:14. "Those who seek Him lack nothing" (Psalm 34:9).

To abide is to seek Him above everything else. "Seek first his kingdom," (Matt. 6:33). Everything else is gravy. But what does it mean to "seek first"? Does it mean to pray and have your quiet time early every morning, then check Him off your list and go on with the rest of the day? Jean Fleming said: "Seeking God first is not a matter of order, but of focus. Christ must not become simply another item in our life—not even the most important item. He did not come in order to be the most crucial piece of our fragmented life: He came to absorb all of life—our family, job, talents, dreams, ministry—into Himself and impress on it His mark."[14]

To abide is to know that whatever happens—expected or unexpected, welcome or unwelcome—the essential thing is to stay connected to the Vine. It is to want His presence more than your own security. To feel His blood pulse in your veins, His heart beat in your chest. To abide is to watch for His hand behind the fabric of life—the hand you have held until you know each line and each callous by heart. To abide is to be able to hear the voice of your one Great Love, to pick it out from all the others in the room.

🕯 My heart has heard you say, "Come and talk with me, O my people." And my heart responds, "Lord, I am coming" (Psalm 27:8 TLB).

CHAPTER 7

Follow Me

Come, follow me.

—Matthew 4:19

To put it bluntly, people have had their bellyful of our sermonizing. They want a source of strength for their lives. We can recommend it only by making it actively present in our own.

—Brennan Manning[1]

I've been thinking about following. Other than Jesus, who asks me to follow them, and what do they expect of me?

I follow a guide who leads me down a trail or steers me through river rapids. An usher escorts me to my seat in the theater; a docent tours me through a museum. I follow a nurse through the tangle of corridors to the examining room. A receptionist points me toward the right office. A hostess seats me at my table.

They expect me to, well, follow. They expect me to trust that they know the way. I doubt they would expect for me to argue with them about the directions. I asked them to lead me because they have been there before and they know where I should go.

So Jesus tells us to follow Him. Everywhere life leads us, He has been there before. Every circumstance, every emotion, every pain and every joy, every height, and every depth, He has walked them. He knows the way. "For we do not have a high priest who is unable to sympathize with our weaknesses," reasons Hebrews 4:15–16, "but we have one who has been tempted in every way, just as we are—yet was without sin. Let us then approach the throne of grace with confidence, so that we may receive mercy and find grace to help us in our time of need."

I like that the writer called it "the throne of grace," not a throne of power or a throne of holiness—which it is. But it is the throne of One who can sympathize with us. When we feel like oddballs in this world, He smiles sympathetically. When we wrestle with God's will, He nods in understanding. "Gethsemane," He whispers to Himself. When we are alone and afraid, He shudders with recognition: "Calvary."

"I am astonished that you are so quickly deserting the one who called you by the grace of Christ," Paul wrote to the Galatians (Gal. 1:6). When a Christian deserts the grace of God, he deserts the God of grace—and this, Paul said, is no gospel at all (v. 7).

The church is in danger of becoming paralyzed in the grip of self-sufficiency. We meet, we discuss, we poll, we argue, we vote. We cut the kingdom work down to a size we deem manageable. We while away hours in committees, devising plans and creating presentations to ensure that everyone understands. The life of faith is not a life in which everyone understands! It is a life in which everybody picks up their tents when God says, "Go."

I am not ignorant of the effort involved in moving hundreds of people in one direction. I am a minister's wife! God ordains order in His body. But the church is not a corporation; it is a community of faith. How will we ever witness God's miraculous ability if we do not venture beyond our own understanding? And where will our neighbors see it demonstrated, if not in us? We are meant to be a mysterious, supernatural community in which the inexplicable is a constant occurrence. As long as we can credit human ability, we have achieved only human results. People may be impressed by us, but they will not be drawn to God.

John Wimber, the late pastor and founder of The Vineyard churches, recalled his early experiences in the community of believers.[2]

> "When do I get to do the stuff?" I kept asking.
> "What stuff?" the church members replied.
> "You know, the stuff Jesus did—healing,
>   miracles—that stuff," I said.
> "Oh, we don't do that stuff," the members said.
>   "We believe in it, but we don't actually do it."
> "Oh, man!" I sighed, highly disappointed.
>   "I gave up drugs for this?"

Meanwhile, the communities of commerce and industry go out on limbs as thin as twigs to accomplish their purposes. The disciples of Weight Watchers, Stephen Covey, Little League, and E-trade are more disciplined in their commitment than Christ's followers. Why? Because their gods are more reliable to deliver than ours? Certainly not. But perhaps because they are more confident that their gods will deliver. Every day by our private and corporate behavior we deliver the message that our God is not trustworthy. God will call us to account for this. Meanwhile, our half-hearted commitment to Christ is not much of a recommendation to others. The gospel itself is enough of a stumbling block, without our complicating its message. Manning says:

> Philosopher William James said: "In some people religion exists as a dull habit, in others as an acute fever." Jesus did not endure the shame of the cross to hand on a dull habit. (If you don't have the fever, dear reader, a passion for God and his Christ, drop this

book, fall on your knees, and beg for it; turn to the God you half-believe in and cry out for his baptism of fire.).

I am not speaking of multiplying altars and sacrifices or plunging into a series of spiritual activities or lengthening the time of formal prayer or getting involved in more church-related organizations. I am not speaking of fasts, rituals, devotions, liturgies, or prayer meetings. I am speaking of a life lived completely for God, the astonishing life of a committed disciple who is willing to follow Jesus . . . a life of surrender without reservation. I propose it in humility and boldness. I mean this literally, completely; I mean it for you and me.[3]

"Do you love me?" Jesus asked Peter (John 21). Jesus used the word *agape*, meaning the godly kind of love that would cause a person to die for another. It would require this kind of furious, all-consuming love for Christ to go where Peter would be led. Peter didn't understand it at the time, having just denied Jesus three times. But Christ would lead Peter to that kind of love.

"Delight is a higher tribute than duty," writes John Piper.[4] We follow Him at first out of curiosity, fear, or even duty. But we stick with Him because we love Him. Love is both the motivation and the resulting fruit of our commitment. When my pastor, Mike Glenn, performs a wedding ceremony, he often asks the couple, "Can you keep a promise?" He then goes on to say:

The laughter of the people behind you gives you a hint that when they were standing here, they had no idea of the promises they were making. And the truth is, there is no way for you to know what you are about to do, where your life will take you, what your marriage will look like. Your journey will be very different from my journey, from the journey of your parents. Your family will be very different from any of those in this sanctuary.

So, I guess here is the question I really want you to answer: Can you keep a promise, even when the circumstances change? Oh sure, it's very easy to stand here in front of your friends in this beautiful sanctuary and tell each other that you will love each other to the end of the world. But what about when the circumstances change?

(To the groom): You have told me that she is the most beautiful woman in the world. But what happens that afternoon when you come home from work, and she is still wearing her robe from that morning, plus what the baby didn't like for lunch. Will you find a way to step over the toys, walk over to her, cup her face in your hands, and tell her she is the most beautiful woman you have ever seen? Can you keep a promise even when the situation changes?

(To the bride): You have told me that he is your hero. But what happens when he is not heroic, when he fails, when he blows it, when he hurts so badly there are no words to tell you, only tears? Will he still be your hero? Even in the times when he is not heroic? Can you keep your promise even when the situation is very, very different?

For better or for worse, in sickness and in health. Just as in marriage, our faithfulness is the proof of our love for Christ. Our ability to keep our promise is our credential.

Some of Jesus' early disciples were followers of John the Baptist (John 1:24–37). Why did these disciples leave John to go after

Jesus? Because John told them to. They trusted John. Consider the audacity required for us to say to someone, "You should believe in Christ." They will look at us and ask why. They will look at our lives for proof.

"Let your gentleness be evident to all. The Lord is near. Do not be anxious about anything," Paul exhorted the Philippians (4:5–6). Let your relaxed life be evidence that God is near. How does your life hold up as evidence?

When the persecuted New Testament believers heard the message, "The Lord is near," it was good news. If the Lord was close at hand in time and place, then a new kingdom was about to come. Perhaps they didn't entirely comprehend this new kingdom, but they recognized it as a better world. I am not sure that we do.

You've probably heard the story of Mildred's funeral. Mildred, being advanced in years, decided to set her affairs in order. She went to see her pastor to discuss her funeral arrangements. After they had met, the pastor said, "Well, Mildred, I think you have given me everything right down to the last detail."

"There's just one more thing," Mildred said. "I would like to be buried with a fork in my hand."

"I beg your pardon?" replied the preacher.

"A fork," nodded Mildred. "I would like to be buried with a fork in my hand."

The preacher scratched his head. "May I ask why?"

"I've eaten many Sunday dinners in my lifetime," Mildred explained, "and when the dishes are cleared to make way for dessert, everyone always says, 'Keep your fork. The best is yet to come.' Since I will have an open-casket funeral, I want everyone who sees me to remember one thing: Keep your fork. The best is yet to come."

"Let us fix our eyes on Jesus," said the writer of Hebrews, "who *for the joy set before Him* endured the cross . . . .Consider Him . . . so that you will not grow weary and lose heart" (12:2–3, italics mine). We will lose heart if we forget that this world is not our final destination.

The best is yet to come. We are headed where Jesus was headed.

In the parable of the seed and the sower, the "seed that fell among the thorns" is the man who hears the good news, but the worries of this life choke it, making it unfruitful (Matt. 13:22). And that's what happens to the fruit of joy in our lives when we are so encumbered by this world that we forget that it's only temporary. Suppose I could tell you for sure that Jesus will come tomorrow. Would that be joyous news? Or have you already started making a list of all the things that need to be done before He gets here?

Jesus will come tomorrow—and today. He is here now, in every moment asking us to follow, to walk lightly in this world, with our hearts set on the next. Following Jesus produces in us the pleasing fruit of joy and faith. "Now faith is being sure of what we hope for and certain of what we do not see" (Heb. 11:1). Faith is being certain that the kingdom to come is the "real world," the one that matters—so certain, that we live by the values of the future world, even as we dwell in the present one.

When the children of Israel were led out of Egypt, they followed God in the form of a cloud by day and a pillar of fire by night. God's presence with them was so tangible it hung over their camp as a thick cloud. When the cloud lifted and moved on, the Israelites moved on. I'm sure there were one or two Israelites who got tired of pulling up stakes and packing. Maybe they'd grown to like the way the valley curved just beyond their tent; maybe the tomato vines they'd planted were producing nicely. "How can we be sure there is a Promised Land?" they wondered. "Maybe Moses doesn't know what he's talking about." So when the time came to move on, they decided to stay put. They waved good-bye to their neighbors and sat down in their rockers and sighed, "Home sweet home."

But when the last of their friends and relations had wound their way out of sight, the valley began to feel lonely. They ate the last of their tomato harvest, and they sat in their rockers, and they said,

"You know, things just aren't the way they were in the old days." Here is the lesson for you and me: No matter how good life is in one place and time, when the Spirit of God says "Move on," nothing will ever be the same—because the place to be is where God is. That is true for both this world and the next. So make camp; spread out your tents. But drive your stakes in lightly. Accumulate little. Make short lists, and don't sweat it so much when it all doesn't get done. Keep your focus on the Real World, because this one will wear you out. The best is yet to come, and you are meant to be living proof of that.

After my initial bout with panic attacks, while I was confined to rest, friends and church members would come to visit me. They would bring casseroles, and they would sit on the edge of my bed and tell me, "I am so relieved to know that you can't keep up, because I am having trouble, too." It wasn't a relief to me. It was an embarrassment and a lesson I didn't particularly want to learn, especially in front of my peers. Especially when I had established myself as such a "pillar of the church." "Satan has asked to sift you as wheat," Jesus told Peter. "But I have prayed for you, Simon, that your faith may not fail. And when you have turned back, strengthen your brothers" (Luke 22:31–32). Perhaps the lesson I am learning is not just for me. That's why I am sharing it with you.

"A piece of writing requires at least two people: one to write it and one to read it. Who's going to read yours?" Patricia O'Connor challenges would-be writers.[5] I've asked myself this question in writing this book. I imagine there are some "pillars of the church" reading this book. I wonder if you are as weary as I was. I wonder if anyone suspects. I wonder if you are doing yourself or anyone else a favor by keeping your weaknesses a secret.

One of the friends who sat on my bed is Amie. I watch her life, and I know she is in danger of ending up in my condition. (I can say this to you because I have said it to her.) Where did Amie learn her busy-for-God lifestyle? She learned it from me. Where did I learn it? From you. Many of you who read this book are ones in whose footsteps I've followed. I've looked to you to learn to be strong, to carry my share of the load, to do my duty. I've learned to admire fortitude. I've learned to applaud capability. I've learned to work wholeheartedly. But I was not given permission to sit down.

"Watch your life and doctrine closely," Paul advised Timothy. "Persevere in them, because if you do, you will save both yourself and your hearers" (1 Tim. 4:16). Beth Moore introduced me to a profound excerpt on this subject, taken from comedienne Gilda Radner's book *It's Always Something*:

> When I was little, my nurse Dibby's cousin had a dog, just a mutt, and the dog was pregnant. I don't know how long dogs are pregnant, but she was due to have her puppies in about a week. She was out in the yard one day and got in the way of the lawn mower, and her two hind legs got cut off. They rushed her to the vet and he said, "I can sew her up, or you can put her to sleep if you want, but the puppies are okay. She'll be able to deliver the puppies."
>
> Dibby's cousin said, "Keep her alive."
>
> So the vet sewed up her backside, and over the next week the dog learned to walk. She didn't spend any time worrying, she just learned to walk by taking two steps in the front and flipping up her backside, and then taking two steps and flipping up her backside again. She gave birth to six little puppies, all in perfect health. She nursed them and then weaned them. And when they learned to walk, they all walked like her.[6]

"Follow my example, as I follow the example of Christ," Paul instructed the new believers (1 Cor. 11:1). How would others walk if they learned to walk like you? I have always aspired to be a leader, but I am becoming less concerned with being a good leader and more concerned with being a good follower. It is a better legacy, I think. Hebrews 12:12–13 encourages me in this: "So take a new grip with your tired hands and stand firm on your shaky legs. Mark out a straight path for your feet. Then those who follow you, though they are weak and lame, will not stumble and fall but will become strong" (NLT).

"When I grow up, I want to be just like you," Amie once said to me. This scares me, especially as I see her indeed following in my footsteps. It is flattering to be chosen as a role model. But I am afraid I have not taught her how desperately I need God in order to live the life she admires.

Our ancestry is not of strong, sure, efficient people, but of rascals, whiners, idolaters, bunglers, backsliders, and backstabbers. How has the kingdom of God moved forward? Literally by the grace of God. We would fling open the floodgates of mercy if we would let go of our self-sufficiency. If we would take our finger out of the dike, God's power would flood the community of faith, and the church would become "a city on a hill that cannot be hidden." We would light the world. It would be scary, yes. But it would not be boring, and we would not grow weary.

These are radical propositions. It requires no less than a radical devotion to Jesus Christ in order to follow where He leads. I fall short every day. So do you. In a stunning lyric, the young Christian songwriter Kyle Matthews expresses this:

> Cursing every step of the way, he bore a heavy load
> To the market ten miles away, the journey took its toll
> And every day he passed a monastery's high cathedral walls
> And it made his life seem meaningless and small

And he wondered how it would be to live in such a place
To be warm, well fed and at peace, to shut the world away
So when he saw a priest who walked, for once, beyond the
    iron gate
He said, "Tell me of your life inside that place"

And the priest replied . . .
We fall down, we get up
We fall down, we get up
We fall down, we get up
And the saints are just the sinners
Who fall down . . . and get up.[7]

A church in our community has hung a banner across the side of its building. The banner reads, "Sinners and backsliders welcome." I applaud their boldness and authenticity. And their accuracy—for this is the good news of Jesus Christ: We can get up and go on again. It is not too late. God changes churches by changing each one of us. So let us look away from all else but Jesus. Let us not allow ourselves to become fatigued in producing what is pleasing to God, for in God's own time, He will produce in us a harvest that is beautiful, if we do not fall apart and dissolve.

I will pray for you. Pray for me.

> May the God of peace, who through the blood of the eternal covenant brought back from the dead our Lord Jesus, that great Shepherd of the sheep, equip you with everything good for doing his will, and may he work in us what is pleasing to him, through Jesus Christ, to whom be glory for ever and ever. Amen (Heb. 13:20–21).

NOTES

Introduction: Growing Weary in Doing Good

[1]Flora Wuellner, *Prayer and the Living Christ* (Nashville: Abingdon, 1969), 12.

[2]Dallas Willard, *The Spirit of the Disciplines: Understanding How God Changes Lives* (San Francisco: Harper and Row,, 1988), 1, 12.

[3]Brennan Manning, *The Signature of Jesus* (Sisters, OR: Multnomah Books, 1996), 197.

[4]Diane Ball, "In His Time" (Nashville: Maranatha! Music, 1978).

[5]John Piper, *Let the Nations Be Glad! The Supremacy of God in Missions* (Grand Rapids: Baker Books, 1993), 30.

[6]Beth Moore, *Breaking Free: Making Liberty in Christ a Reality in Life* (Nashville: LifeWay, 1999), 124.

[7]*The Book of Common Prayer,* 1979 edition (New York: Seabury Press, 1979), 137.

[8]Oswald Chambers, *My Utmost for His Highest: An Updated Edition in Today's Language* (Grand Rapids: Discover House, 1992), April 13.

[9]Edith Schaeffer, *Common Sense Christian Living* (Nashville: Thomas Nelson, 1983,) 111.

[10]Sue Bender, *Everyday Sacred: A Woman's Journey Home* (New York: HarperCollins, 1995), 39.

Chapter 1: Come to Me, All Who Are Weary

[1]Oswald Chambers, *My Utmost for His Highest* (Grand Rapids: Discovery House, 1992), June 11.

[2]*International Inductive Study Bible,* NIV (Eugene, OR: Harvest House Publishers, 1995), Footnote, 1203.

[3]Chambers, *My Utmost for His Highest,* April 23.

[4]Brennan Manning, *The Signature of Jesus* (Sisters, OR: Multnomah Books, 1996), 197.
[5]Jean Fleming, *Living the Christ-centered Life: Between Walden and the Whirlwind* (Colorado Springs, CO: NavPress, 1985), 50.
[6]Manning, *The Signature of Jesus,* 16.

Chapter 2: Consider Him, So That You Do Not Grow Weary

[1]Kathleen Norris, *Amazing Grace: A Vocabulary of Faith* (New York: Riverhead Books, 1998), 360.
[2]John Piper, *Let the Nations Be Glad! The Supremacy of God in Missions* (Grand Rapids: Baker Books, 1993), 221.
[3]Brennan Manning, *The Signature of Jesus* (Sisters, OR: Multnomah Books, 1996, 28–29.
[4]Manning, *The Signature of Jesus,* 22.
[5]The best list I have found is in the appendix pages of *Experiencing God* by Henry Blackaby and Claude V. King (Nashville: Broadman & Holman, 1990).
[6]Oswald Chambers, *My Utmost for His Highest* (Grand Rapids: Discover House, 1992), April 9.
[7]Norris, *Amazing Grace: A Vocabulary of Faith,* 162.

Chapter 3: Growing Weary in Worship

[1]Warren W. Wiersbe, *Real Worship: It Will Transform Your Life* (Nashville: Oliver-Nelson, 1986), 41.
[2]John Piper, *Let The Nations Be Glad! The Supremacy of God in Missions* (Grand Rapids: Baker Books, 1993), 11.
[3]Lillian Hellman, *Pentimento* (New York: Little Brown & Co., 1973).
[4]Beth Moore, *Breaking Free: Making Liberty in Christ a Reality in Life* (Nashville: LifeWay Press, 1999), 14.
[5]Sue Bender, *Everyday Sacred: A Woman's Journey Home* (New York: HarperCollins, 1995), 9.
[6]Dominique Voillaume, diaries as quoted by Brennan Manning

in *The Signature of Jesus* (Sisters, OR: Multnomah Books, 1996), 104.

[7]Jean Fleming, *Living the Christ-centered Life Between Walden and the Whirlwind* (Colorado Springs: NavPress, 1985), 100.

[8]Edith Schaeffer, *Common Sense Christian Living* (Nashville: Thomas Nelson, 1983), 91.

Chapter 4: Growing Weary in Obedience
[1]Brennan Manning, *The Signature of Jesus* (Sisters, OR: Multnomah Books, 1996), 194.

[2]G. Campbell Morgan, as quoted by Warren W. Wiersbe in *Real Worship* (Nashville: Oliver-Nelson, 1986), 11.

[3]Henry Blackaby and Claude V. King, *Experiencing God* (Nashville: Broadman & Holman, 1990), 136.

[4]Manning, *The Signature of Jesus,* 191.

[5]Beth Moore, *Breaking Free: Making Liberty in Christ a Reality in Life* (Nashville: LifeWay, 1999), 45.

[6]Manning, *The Signature of Jesus,* 179.

Chapter 5: Growing Weary Without Truth
[1]C.S. Lewis, *The Voyage of the Dawn Treader* (New York: HarperCollins, 1980), 91, 107–9.

[2]Gail Godwin, *Evensong* (New York: Ballantine Books, 1999).

[3]Warren W. Wiersbe, *Real Worship* (Nashville: Oliver-Nelson, 1986), 31.

[4]Esther Burroughs, as quoted by Karla Worley in *Glimpses of Christ in Everyday Lives* (Birmingham, AL: New Hope Publishers, 1998), 205.

Chapter 6: Growing Weary Without Abiding
[1]Corrie Ten Boom, *This New Day*, quoted by Margaret D. Smith in *Journal Keeper* (Grand Rapids: Eerdmans, 1993), 36.

[2]Sue Bender, *Everyday Sacred: A Woman's Journey Home* (New

York: HarperCollins, 1995), 27.

[3]Oswald Chambers, *My Utmost for His Highest* (Grand Rapids: Discovery House, 1992), January 6.

[4]Jean Fleming, *Living the Christ-centered Life Between Walden and the Whirlwind* (Colorado Springs: NavPress, 1985), 99.

[5]Ralph Waldo Emerson, as quoted by Smith in *Journal Keeper*, 90.

[6]Catherine Marshall, as quoted by Edith Schaeffer in *The Art of Life* (Westchester, IL: Crossway Books, 1987), 7.

[7]Bender, *Everyday Sacred*, 38.

[8]Edith Schaeffer, *Common Sense Christian Living* (Nashville: Thomas Nelson, 1983), 225.

[9]Schaeffer, *Common Sense Christian Living*, 226–7

[10]Karla Worley, "Praying the Wrong Prayer," *Missions Mosaic*, July 1997, 8.

[11]Edith Schaeffer, *Common Sense Christian Living*, 227.

[12]Bender, *Everyday Sacred*, 13.

[13]Rosalie Beck, "A Listening Heart," *Missions Mosaic*, November 1999, 44.

[14]Fleming, *Living the Christ-centered Life Between Walden and the Whirlwind*, 23.

Chapter 7: Follow Me

[1]Brennan Manning, *The Signature of Jesus* (Sisters, OR: Multnomah Books, 1996), 196.

[2]Excerpted from an interview with Peter Jennings (New York: ABC News).

[3]Manning, *The Signature of Jesus*, 95–6.

[4]John Piper, *Let the Nations Be Glad! The Supremacy of God in Missions* (Grand Rapids: Baker Books, 1993), 219.

[5]Patricia O'Connor, *Words Fail Me* (New York: Harcourt Brace & Co., 1999), 12.

[6]Gilda Radner, *It's Always Something* (New York: Avon Books, 1989), 268–9.

[7]Kyle Matthews, "We Fall Down," (1998 BMG Songs, Inc./Above The Rim Music, administered by BMG Songs, Inc./ASCAP). Used by permission.

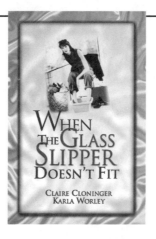

Also by Karla Worley
cowritten with Claire Cloninger

For every woman whose *life isn't what she expected,* here's help—and even a *smile.*

Claire Cloninger and **Karla Worley** speak with warmth and candor to women living in the everyday world. Filled with advice on accepting our bodies (stretch marks and all), finding fulfillment in life's chores (from laundry to boardroom presentations), and loving our husbands (though they didn't come from the same gene pool as Prince Charming), this is every woman's guide to accepting life's realities gracefully and celebrating the journey we call womanhood.

Available from your local Christian bookstore.

New Hope® Publishers